Not Sure Where I'm Going But I'm Making Great Time

Ken Pelton

Copyright © 2019 by Ken Pelton
All rights reserved
Edited by Heather Cunningham and Ted Pelton
ISBN 9781797964836
Printed in the United States of America

Acknowledgments

I owe a huge thank you to my loving daughter, Lee, for encouraging me to write this book and helping through the long grieving process after Kathy, her mother and my lifetime love passed away on October 5^{th,} 2017. I would have been a basket case without her love and support.

I also want to thank, my nephew, Ted Pelton, Ph.D., Chair of English literature at Tenessee Tech University and Heather Cunningham, my sweet granddaughter for their help on my manuscript.

A Note to Readers

This story, about my September 2003 motorcycle adventure sat inside my computer for 15 years. It is based on my very detailed handwritten journaling sometimes done several times a day during rest-stops at roadside parks and restaurants, but mostly at the end of the day in motel rooms when the conversations and emotions were still vivid in my mind.

I titled the book, "Not Sure Where I'm Going, but I'm making Good Time" because my daily destinations were largely made up based on spur-of-the-moment decisions. That has always been my preferred way to travel because it offers more spontaneity and surprises. I like that.

I have dedicated this book to Kathy, my lifetime love. Sadly, my sweet Kathy died on October 5th, 2017 from a very aggressive form of cancer. I was lucky in love, marrying a beautiful, sweet 20-year-old girl that throughout our 53 years of marriage encouraged me to follow my dreams. One of those dreams involved my love of motorcycles and motorcycle travel-adventures.

Kathy and I were fortunate to have done a lot of traveling during our time together. In addition to many trips outside the US, from 2007 to 2010 we toured the US and Canada with our RV and our two greyhounds, often for several months at a time. We had a wonderful life together.

From our home in Cooper City (near Fort Lauderdale), Florida I was able to take five cross-country motorcycle trips between 1995 and 2012. This involved three roundtrips to the California coast and two rides out to the westerner states and up to Canada through Montana and back. Kathy flew out west and accompanied me for two of these trips.

With that said, the ride I thought most interesting was the 2003 trip and parts of the 1997 trip which are the basis of this book. With some regrets, I sold the Honda Blackbird in 2005. Then, in 2012, to celebrate my 70th birthday, I got the urge once again, so I bought a 2010 Yamaha FJR 1300 and took a ride to the California Coast. The following year I made another trip to Glazer National Park on the Canadian border. The FJR was, by conventional measures a better bike than the blackbird. It had an adjustable windscreen, built-in hard saddlebags, a driveshaft that never needed oiling or replacing, ABS brakes and more, but it was heavier and lacked the rawness and perfect handling of my Blackbird.

    I always had the feeling my Blackbird needed me as much as I needed her. We had a symbiotic relationship and this added an additional layer of excitement, frustration and unpredictability to our travels together. You will see what I mean as you get into the story. Of the nine motorcycles I owned at various times, the Blackbird was, by far, my favorite. If it is possible to have a love affair with a motorcycle, that was my baby.

    Lastly, I should add that Kathy and I have been vegans since 1985 for ethical reasons. In my story, I often use the word vegetarian when dealing with wait-staff in restaurants because many people, particularly in rural areas, don't know what "vegan" means.

    Finally, in my original journaling and in this book I have gone to great effort to tell this story as it happened without added hype or fake drama. Names have been changed to protect the privacy of the people involved. I hope you enjoy the read!

Ken Pelton, Cooper City, FL Email: kenKathy2@bellsouth.net.

Contents

Page   1   Day 1, Leave home, Arrive Titusville, Florida
Page   7   Day 2, Arrive at Florida Panhandle Camp Site
Page   11: Day 3, Arrive Mobile, Alabama
Page   15: Day 4, Arrive Natchez, Mississippi
Page   18: Day 5, Arrive Dumas, Arkansas
Page   23: Day 6, Arrive Oklahoma City, Oklahoma
Page   27: Day 7, Arrive Tucumcari, New Mexico
Page   36: Day 8, Arrive Gallup, New Mexico
Page   41: Day 9, Arrive Freedonia, Arizona
Page   44: Day 10, Arrive Los Vegas, Nevada
Page   47: Day 11, Arrive Ridgecrest, California
Page   50: Dad 12, Arrive San Luis Obispo, California
Page   54: Day 13, Arrive Santa Cruz, California
Page   68: Day 14, Arrive Fairfield, California
Page   75: Day 15, Arrive Bishop, California
Page   80: Day 16, Arrive, Saint George, Utah
Page   97: Day 17, Arrive Escalante, Utah
Page 101: Day 18, Arrive Moab, Utah
Page 106: Day 19, Arrive Provo, Utah
Page 111: Day 20, Arrive Richfield, Utah
Page 117: Day 21, Arrive Flagstaff, Arizona
Page 123: Day 22, Arrive Lordsburg, New Mexico
Page 128: Day 23, Arrive Marfa, Texas
Page 138: Day 24, Arrive Del Rio, Texas
Page 142: Day 25, Arrive San Antonio, Texas
Page 155: Day 26, Arrive Beaumont, Texas
Page 156: Day 27, Arrive Gulfport, Alabama (motorcycle repairs)
Page 159: Day 28, Stayover Gulfport, Alabama (motorcycle repairs)
Page 163: Day 29, Arrive Tallahassee, Florida
Page 166: Day 30, Arrive Home

Thursday, August 28, 2003
Day one: Arrive Titusville, Florida

After a scary motorcycle dream, I sit up in bed. It's 8AM. Kathy's side of the bed is empty. How did I sleep so long? Today, I leave on my third cross-country motorcycle trip in seven years. In the back of my mind, I'm afraid I'll have a nasty accident. That was my dream. I've had a few already, but strangely, it's the close-calls that give me the chills, the things that could have happened but didn't. This trip brings those fears back to the surface. It took me almost two months to work up the courage to make this trip in spite of those annoying fears that manage to push through. Still, I'm excited and anxious to get going.

After rubbing the sleep from my eyes, I put on the cut-offs and T-shirt I left on the floor by the bed last night. No point in putting on clean stuff if I'm just going to be working in the garage. Eddy, my eighty-pound adopted Greyhound, looks up at me from his bed on the floor. "Good morning, Eddy. How's my main man this morning?" He always sleeps until I get up, no matter how late. Kathy's on the family room couch with a cup of coffee, her feet up, reading the morning paper. As usual, the patio door is open to let in the morning sunlight and the pleasant sound of chirping birds from our backyard.

"Today's your big day, Kenny. Did you sleep okay?"

"I guess so, didn't think I'd sleep this late though. Christ, it's already eight o'clock."

After Eddy and I eat breakfast, I walk into the utility room and press the garage door opener to let in some daylight. "I'll be in the garage loading up the bike, Kath," I yell as I walk into the garage with Eddy on my heels. The sun is shining. It's about 78 degrees and the summer morning air feels good on my skin, another beautiful South Florida day. My bike is resting on its center-stand, right where I left it last night after returning from the Honda shop. It's a 1997 Honda Blackbird CBR 1100 XX. When I bought it six years and twenty-eight thousand miles ago, it was billed as the fastest production motorcycle in the world, with a top speed of 175 mph. Since then, I had the carburetor jets bored out and a more efficient after-market exhaust system installed. On a test run a few years ago, I got it up to 188 mph. Now it's fully

Thursday, August 28, 2003
Day one: Arrive Titusville, Florida

prepped with new tires and ready for its second cross-country trip. All I have to do is load on my luggage and camping gear.

Tackling the hardest piece first, I set my coffee cup on my permanently cluttered workbench and fish around for Allan wrenches in my aging tool chest The chest is the sole asset from my younger brother's so-called estate when he died in 1999. Donald was only fifty-three when he lost his battle with throat cancer. The toolbox was my reward for taking care of him during the last two years of his life. Donald's ashes are in a clear plastic bag here in the garage. He's on the shelf just above his toolbox inside a cardboard box marked "Donald" with some of his old photographs and letters. I keep Donny near his toolbox because it was his only and most valued asset. So here his ashes stay, on a storage shelf beside boxes of our old tax records and a deflated basketball.

Anyway, my first job is to install the luggage system I used on my last cross-country trip in 1997. I have to bolt the tubular metal support piece to the rear frame of the bike. I haven't looked at this stuff in six years; now I notice the scratches and dents from the spill I took just east of Yosemite National Park. It was on this same bike. That little bit of recklessness cost me fifteen-hundred dollars in motorcycle repairs and a night in the Bishop, California E.R. They had to brush the dirt and gravel from the road rash on my left ass-cheek and the side of my left knee, then bandage me up.

The damage to the metal support piece is mostly superficial, and it should still work fine if I can just find the special bolts I need to attach it to the bike's frame. I put them away "somewhere," but that was in 1997. Now my mind is blank. I scan the thirty-six clear, plastic trays in my hardware organizer with no luck.

Then, I rummage through boxes of old motorcycle accessories—nothing. In desperation, I yell at Eddy, lying on his favorite old rug, coolly watching me go mad. "DAMN IT EDDY, GET OFF YOUR ASS AND HELP ME FIND THESE BOLTS!" Finally, I give up searching and figure I'll try improvising with some other bolts. In the process of

Thursday, August 28, 2003
Day one: Arrive Titusville, Florida

looking for alternative bolts, something strange happens. I look again in my hardware organizer, this time I see them in a tray labeled "Bolts." Who would have guessed? So far, I've managed to stretch a thirty-minute job into an hour and a half. At this rate, I won't get out of here for another month.

With the luggage system installed, I have a vertical, triangular support frame that looks similar to a passenger backrest commonly seen on Harleys, only with no padding. At its base, is a small metal platform facing rearward. The fabric, waterproof luggage piece slides down over the vertical support frame and rests on the metal platform like a little pup tent. In here, I pack emergency repair tools: a flashlight and extra batteries, duct tape, wire, walking around shoes, flat tire repair kit, rope, a container of personal care items and a first-aid kit. I have a little room left over for a small souvenir or two if I buy any.

Next, I throw a pair of soft saddlebags over the passenger seat. They flop over the sides of the bike and attach to the frame with plastic snap-clips. The saddlebags hold two bath towels, four pairs of jeans, eight T-shirts, eight pairs of socks, a pair of walking shorts and two pairs of underwear that I'll probably never use. In the hot weather, they block cool airflow to a critical body area with an unnecessary layer of clothing. Then, I place a third matching piece of luggage on top of the passenger seat, right between the saddlebags. This stores the cold weather, insulated jacket liner that fits under my ventilated motorcycle jacket; a lightweight, two-piece rain suit; and a heavyweight, one-piece all-weather rain suit.

On top of the gas tank, I attach a tank-bag with a clear plastic top-cover, under which I can slip my roadmap for easy viewing. Inside the tank-bag, I store my pens, camera, cell phone, and a campground directory along with ten packs of pre-moistened ass-wipes. If I'm not wearing underwear, I want to to keep my ass as sanitary as possible. What I don't pack is a pistol, assault rifle, knife, hand grenade, mace, or any other dangerous devices. The motorcycle is dangerous enough. From the corner of my eye, I see Kathy peeking in the garage; she's

Thursday, August 28, 2003
Day one: Arrive Titusville, Florida

taking a break from her housecleaning to see how I'm making out. Her eyes survey the luggage already loaded on the bike. She looks skeptically at the four large items of camping gear still on the garage floor.

"Kathy, you don't think I can get all this stuff on the motorcycle, do you?"

"Well Kenny, it looks like a lot. I don't see how it's all going to fit."

"Okay, just check back in a few minutes and I'll show you how I do it."

I know Kathy has a good point, but I press on, hoping I can make it work. I've decided to camp out on this trip, I bought all the right gear and I'm not going to give up yet. The four pieces of camping gear are sausage-shaped bedrolls, between 18 and 24-inches long, a two-man tent, a sleeping bag, a self-inflating mattress and a rolled up, eight-foot by ten-foot plastic tarp that goes under my tent to keep out the water when it rains. The tent is the heaviest of the four pieces and I lay it sideways, across the passenger seat and over the saddlebags. Next, I load on the remaining three items the same way and secure them to the tubular metal support frame with two nylon cinch straps. I stand back to take a look. Well done, Ken. Then I yell for Kathy, "I'm done! Come take a look!" A moment later, the utility door cracks open. Kathy walks in the garage, puts her hands on her hips with a doubtful expression and says,

"I don't know Kenny, it looks top-heavy to me, how are you going to get your leg over all that stuff?"

"Watch this," and I throw my leg over the luggage and mount the bike like a 25-year-old kid. "See, no problem."

"Are you sure it's safe? I mean can't you tip over with all that stuff?"

"Don't worry Kath, I know exactly what I'm doing. It's fine, really."

Thursday, August 28, 2003
Day one: Arrive Titusville, Florida

By three o'clock in the afternoon, after some lunch and a shower, I'm ready to hit the road. On my last two trips out west, Kathy flew out to meet me and we spent about half of the trip touring together, but this time I'm going solo. Kathy stopped riding as a passenger back in '97. She had a lot of fun and never got hurt, so now she figures why push her luck? I'll be gone for about a month and already, I feel a sense of loss in the pit of my stomach. How can I be homesick already? I miss Kathy and our Greyhound, Eddy, and I haven't even left the house yet.

Standing in the driveway next to the bike, I put on my bravest face, look into Kathy's eyes and give her a big hug. Her eyes fill with tears and she squeezes me hard against her slender body. Our lips meet for a sweet kiss mixed with tears. I knew this time would come, but it's more difficult than I expected.

"Kenny, promise me you'll be careful, that you won't speed and you'll come home in one piece."

"I promise."

"No, I want you to say it out loud, the whole thing."

"Okay, I promise I won't speed, I'll be careful and come home in one piece. Seriously, sweetheart, I'll be good. I swear. The crazy riding is history, I love you very much."

Reluctantly, we break our embrace, I bend down beside Eddy and give him a big hug, "Bye, bye Eddy, you be a good boy and take care of Mommy, okay?" Then I mount the bike, put on my full-face helmet, crank up the engine and wobble out of the driveway. I look back at Kathy and Eddy; they're standing next to each other in the driveway watching me leave. For an instant, I want to go back. We exchange one last farewell wave, and my motorcycle adventure is underway!

Even though the Blackbird is seven years old with 28,000 miles, it still feels tight. The 160-horsepower four-cylinder engine responds like a high-spirited colt. Propelling the 492-pound (dry weight) bike around slower vehicles with no downshifting needed. I feel reborn with a big trip in front of me. First stop: visit and spend the night with my older brother, Bob and his wife, Pat, in Titusville, about two hundred miles

Thursday, August 28, 2003
Day one: Arrive Titusville, Florida

north. The Florida Turnpike is a dull ride, but in spite of that, it's invigorating to be on the road.

When I left my neighborhood, I noticed, just as Kathy observed, the bike feels top-heavy, but only at low speeds. Once on the Turnpike, it feels normal except that the camping gear shifts position, I can see it in my rearview mirrors and it makes me nervous. I stop and check it at the West Palm Beach Service Plaza. It's mainly the tent, the heaviest piece that's moving. I put it back in position and re-tighten the nylon cinch belts. In Fort Pierce, I exit the turnpike to get on I-95 and stop for gas. I adjust the tent...again.

At 7PM, I pull into Bob's place, right on time. Bob's wife, Pat, prepared a tasty rice and black-eyed pea dinner in thoughtful consideration of the longstanding vegan life that Kathy and I share. We talk about my travel plans and our families. Later, after dinner, we get into a testy discussion

about our opposing views on the Iraq war, patriotism and President Bush. Bob and Pat are both staunch, Bush Republicans and I'm an anti-war, tree-hugging liberal. But in spite of our differences, we end the evening on peacefully.

I'm sleeping in their forty-foot motorhome parked under a tall enclosure attached to their house. The motorhome is more like a Marriott hotel room with a large glass enclosed shower, brass faucet handles, marble floor, TV and refrigerator. It's all quite beautiful. After a warm shower, I spend time writing in my journal.

Friday, August 29, 2003
Day Two: Arrive at Florida Panhandle Camp Site

It takes about 10 minutes to get the luggage reloaded and I'm sweating because at 10AM, it's warm, humid and sunny. From Titusville, I get back on I-95 and head north. Traffic is moderate. I want to hit I-10 in Jacksonville then head west across the panhandle of northern Florida. The Florida Panhandle is a long, three hundred and fifty-mile ride. I know the road well. I ate a little oatmeal and toast before saying goodbye to Bob and Pat, and I feel like I'll be hungry again soon. I'm cruising at 90 mph, a little faster than the flow of traffic so I don't need to be too concerned about vehicles coming up behind me.

Before I left, I bought a new ventilated, armored jacket with matching ventilated gloves and a full-face helmet, all color coordinated in yellow and black, to go with my black bike. Outwardly, it makes my 5-foot, 10-inch, 150-pound body look and feel deceptively young, that is, until I take off the helmet and see my 60-year-old baldhead and short white beard in the men's room mirror. Threading through and around slower vehicles, I reflect on last night's discussion with Bob and Pat. I'm against Bush's policies and adamantly against the war. Kathy and I marched in three war protest rallies.

"I back the president," Bob told me, "I love this country, it's the greatest country in the world, and we have to protect it."

"I don't buy it, Bob. I supported the first Iraq war, but there's no proof Iraq had anything to do with Al Qaeda or 9/11. The flag waving and the blind faith in Bush is all bullshit. Ever since this war started, everyone in America is running around with flags on their cars; it turns me off." That kind of killed the conversation for the evening.

As I hit Jacksonville, the heat and humidity are weighing on me and the camping gear still has an annoying way of sliding around, now it's moving forward and pushing against my lower back. I recall Kathy telling me I have too much luggage as I reach behind me to push it back into position, but this causes me to inadvertently change lanes. Very dangerous. I need gas, so I pull over at a gas station. In spite of Kathy's remarks about my luggage, I still believe I can get the camping gear positioned and tied down properly; I just need to find the optimum arrangement. While I'm drinking some water, I pull my campground

Friday, August 29, 2003
Day Two: Arrive at Florida Panhandle Camp Site

directory out of my tank bag and locate a five-star campground just off I-10, east of Pensacola. With my cell phone, I call and make reservations for tent space. It's almost a three-hundred-mile ride, but it's noon and I think I can make it there by 5PM.

At 2PM, I look at the sky. It's getting dark and I smell rain. At a rest stop, I put on my two-piece rain outfit and adjust the camping gear, hopefully for the last time, because I think I have it just about right now. A few minutes later I hit my first rainfall. It's a soaker. From the looks of the sky, it will last a while. Shit! I forgot about my cell-phone, it's in the side-pouch of my tank-bag and undoubtedly getting wet. I forgot to put it back in its plastic waterproof bag. Oh well, maybe I'll get lucky and it will still work when it dries out. Riding in the rain on a motorcycle is pleasant because I'm wearing a full-face helmet and full-body raingear. It can even give you an illusion of safety because you feel so snug, warm and insulated from the harsh, wet weather.

The rain can be brutal, though, if you don't have your face protected. People in cars never experience the effect of high-speed rain, but motorcycle people know about it. Imagine driving a car with no windshield, the rain hitting your tender unprotected face at 75 mph. Even Arnold Schwarzenegger's "Terminator" couldn't handle the pain. The raindrops feel like a storm of BB gun pellets slamming into your face.

I hit rain one afternoon riding my Harley Soft-Tail Custom heading home from Miami. I had no windscreen and an open-face helmet. When the rain hit my face, I thought it would rip my skin off. I really didn't know what to do. Big Al, my Harley friend, comfortable behind the high, protective windscreen of his big Harley "Dresser" motioned me to pull over.

"That rain smarts a bit, don't it?"

"Yeah, you've got it made behind your car-sized windscreen, I'm dying."

"Here, wrap this around your face," he says, handing me a large white rag from his saddlebag. I tied it across my face like a bandit's

Friday, August 29, 2003
Day Two: Arrive at Florida Panhandle Camp Site

mask and we got back on the road. The rag was just enough to take the pain out of riding in the rain. A couple of years later, three-hundred-pound, Big Al died of a big heart attack. He was one of the most colorful, coolest guys I ever rode with.

It's 4PM and it's been raining for two hours now. I'm wondering if it's going to last all day. I've been riding for six hours and I don't think I'm going to make it to that fancy, five-star campground. I'm getting tired and it's at least an hour away. I don't want to camp out in the rain anyway. Fifteen minutes later, the weather gods feel sorry for me. The rain dries up and the late afternoon sun makes a weak appearance. I stop at the first campground I spot, a KOA about two miles off I-10. At the registration office, I pay the $15 fee and the guy at the desk points to a field on the other side of a narrow gravel road and tells me, "Ride your motorcycle right over there and set-up wherever you like."

It looks like five acres of pine trees, no other tents around. I ride my bike over the soft, wet grass covered with pine needles. As I ride along, I stop and pick up a big woodchip to slip under my kickstand, so it doesn't sink into the water-soaked earth.

Unloading the bike, it dawns on me, my first tent camping experience on the road and it isn't starting out that great. Already, I'm sweating like a pig, mosquitoes are flying all around me and the humidity feels like it's at least 130%. I get my two-person tent set up okay and congratulate myself on having had the foresight to practice this procedure a couple of times on my back patio before I left. I sit down inside, no breeze at all. I wonder…how am I going to sleep in this heat and humidity? I swat at the mosquitoes that got trapped in the tent after I zipped up the insect-proof ventilation panels.

I check the time; it's about 5:30PM. I take off my all-weather motorcycle boots and put on my walking shoes. Ah, that feels better. Then I head to the park office and get directions to town. I only ate that small bowl of oatmeal for breakfast. Now I'm starved and I need gas. The manager says, "When you leave the park, head that way," sticking

Friday, August 29, 2003
Day Two: Arrive at Florida Panhandle Camp Site

his arm out and pointing left. "It's seven miles." With the directions loosely in my mind, I take off and promptly ride eight miles in the wrong direction. I'm now in the middle of nowhere. Once you get off I-10, you quickly find out that most of the Florida Panhandle is undeveloped, just two-lane roads and pine trees.

Now I'm really low on gas. I know this because the reserve light was blinking before I left the campsite. I go back to where I started, get my bearings and take off again…hopefully, in the right direction. Great! I find the town. This is a small place, no real restaurants, just fast food joints, a gas station and some small stores. My best bet is the Subway shop. I order a veggie sub, which fills my belly and buy some gas.

To help me sleep, I buy a paperback novel by Tom Clancy. No reflection on Tom Clancy, any reading puts me to sleep. Then, I ride back to my tent, grab my bag of toiletries, walk over to the community bathroom, take a shower and brush the Subway out of my teeth.

On the way back to my dark, hot, humid tent, I stop by the registration office and ask the manager if I can leave my cell-phone in their air-conditioned office overnight to dry out. "Yeah, no problem," he says. I hope it works tomorrow. I call Kathy from the pay phone and let her know I'm okay, a whopping fifty cents for three minutes all over the country. With my battery powered tent lamp, I update my daily journal, read a few pages from Clancy's book and fall asleep

Saturday, August 30, 2003
Day Three: Arrive Mobile, Alabama

The sun wakes me up at 7AM. Surprisingly, I did get some sleep, shallow but enough. The ground was hard even with my sleeping bag on top of my air mattress. And the air pillow attached to the air mattress sucks because it doesn't move; I can't snuggle with it. The thing just stays in one place. The tent floor is a disaster; it's covered with my luggage, clothes, rain gear, toiletries, shoes, pine needles, leaves and plain old Mother Earth dirt. I'm not a very good housekeeper. I wonder if I made a stupid mistake on this camping decision, because last night when I first sat in the tent, the heat, humidity, mosquitoes and boredom overwhelmed me.

Now I'm annoyed because I can't remember where anything is, but the birds chirping outside soothe me while I fish around in my luggage for some clean jeans, socks, T-shirt, bath towel and my toiletry kit. Ken, you don't have a time problem, relax, take it easy. I finally locate what I need, making a bad mess even worse. I put on my walking shorts, shoes and head over to the community showers. After some time on the toilet and a shower, I feel much better. So, I stop in the main office and get a cup of coffee, two bananas and a cup of OJ. I try my cell phone; it's working again. How about that! Maybe I'll live after all.

Back at the campsite, I break down my tent, repack my gear on the bike…and two and a half hours after waking up, I ride out of the park into what is starting out as an oppressively humid day. At last, I'm on the narrow two-lane road leading to I-10. The warm, morning breeze pouring through the ventilation pin holes in my motorcycle jacket evaporate the sweat from my chest…it feels good. On I-10 West, I set my cruising speed at about 90-95 mph and enjoy the ride. I don't worry much about cops, because I'm not weaving between cars. I just stay in whichever lane has the least amount of traffic. The morning ride is pleasant, but around noontime, it gets overbearingly hot and I can't get enough fresh air through the built-in air vents in my helmet. They become more like a cruel joke. I try cracking open my face shield to let in some fresh air, but the wind just slams it shut.

Alabama! Congratulations, Ken! You're finally out of Florida! I pull over at the first rest stop, drink some water and relax on a picnic

Saturday, August 30, 2003
Day Three: Arrive Mobile, Alabama

bench while I write in my journal and figure out a way to get some fresh airflow in my helmet at cruising speed. I roll up a piece of duct tape and stick it in-between the clear plastic face-shield and the bottom edge of the helmet opening. Now when the wind forces my face-shield to close, there will still be a quarter-inch-opening to let in some fresh air.

Hey, why not try to locate another camping site for tonight while I have time? I pull the campground directory from my tank-bag and soon realize I'm wasting my time because I don't know this area well enough to relate to the addresses in the directory. I'll have to play it by ear. Back on I-10, the duct tape keeps the face-shield cracked open and the fresh air feels great. That doesn't keep my old antagonist, the camping gear, from poking me in the back again. It's sliding forward just like yesterday. I'm still trying to convince myself I'll find the magic adjustment and this problem will go away. When am I going to start having fun?

I spot the Alabama Visitor's Center and stop for suggestions on a campsite. The matronly attendant says, "I'd recommend the one just about eight miles south of Mobile off I-10."

"Okay, thanks, I'll try that one." She writes down the name and address and gives it to me. Walking back to my bike, the rain starts again. I put on my rain gear. I don't mind the drizzle, but as I enter Mobile, the spray from the 18-wheelers makes it hard to see through my face-shield. Good, there's Route 22. Following the directions from the lady at the Visitor's Center, I head south on a busy, two-lane road through little towns with dreary colored buildings, old houses used car lots and old trailer parks. Where the hell is the campground? I loop around the tiny town twice, trying to zero in on the address the lady gave me. After eliminating all my options but one, I take a narrow and lonely dirt road to nowhere. There it is! I pull in and spot the manager puttering around in the carport next to his home/office. From my bike, I ask, "Can I set up my tent here for the night?"

"Sorry fella, this place doesn't accept tent campers." Now I'm pissed.

Saturday, August 30, 2003
Day Three: Arrive Mobile, Alabama

"Fuck this!" I say to myself out loud. By the time I get back to I-10, I'll have ridden 16-miles out of my way in rainy weather only to be turned away and now it looks like thunderstorms. Sure enough, five minutes later, all hell breaks loose and I realize camping out in this weather would be insane. It's finally time to change over to plan B. I'm heading back to I-10 and staying in the first cheap motel I see. Then, I'm getting rid of this goddamn camping gear; it's driving me crazy. It makes my bike handle like a pregnant duck and camping out sucks. I'm also thinking, Kathy knew all this from the start. If I weren't such a macho jerk, I would've listened to her female logic.

    I locate an Econo-Lodge in Mobile, Alabama off I-10 for 45-bucks, The Labor Day weekend rate. I'm not in the mood to shop for price. It feels like the Hilton after my rough night in the tent. It occurs to me that maybe I was a bit of a pussy, giving up on the camping thing after only one night, but it just isn't any fun. Besides, this is supposed to be a vacation, not a pleasure deprivation experiment. I feel much better now that I won't be camping-out anymore. It's too time-consuming with long walks to the toilet and showers, shitty sleeping conditions and all the time it takes to set up the tent then break it down and repack everything back on the bike. Too much.

    I decide to leave all the camping stuff in the motel room when I check out. I'm sure someone will find a use for it. After a shower, I head out for something to eat. On the way out, I stop by the front office and ask the young Pakistani desk manager if he would like some free camping gear; he looks at me like, "What's camping?"

    "Thank you, but no," he says. I tell him it's free, but I don't think he believes me. He thinks my offer is too strange.

    "OK," I say and get on the bike to find a restaurant. By now the rain has stopped. It's still light when I find a little family-owned Mexican restaurant and order a veggie burrito. The young waitress speaks broken English and gives me an expression that says, "What's a veggie burrito?" So, I think a moment and say,

    "You know the vegetables you put in a Fajita?"

Saturday, August 30, 2003
Day Three: Arrive Mobile, Alabama

"Yes, yes," she smiles.

"Good, take those same vegetables and wrap them up in a burrito, okay?"

"Okay," she smiles again like she's really with me now. Then, I add

"No carne and no cheese."

"No cheese?" she asks.

This part throws her; she can't understand the "no cheese" thing, so I confirm, "No cheese."

"Okay, no meat and no cheese," she repeats to confirm. Then, she smiles and walks away. The meal is great. After I eat, I have a choice of going to the strip-joint across the street or the local Dollar General store. I choose the Dollar General and wonder if this is another worrisome sign of old age?

Because of all the rain, I buy some extra plastic kitchen garbage bag liners. I put my clothes inside the garbage bag liners and put them in my not-so-waterproof saddlebags. Presto! No wet clothes. I also buy some clothespins. I'm going to try clipping one on the bottom edge of my clear plastic face shield to keep it wedged open enough to let in a little fresh air. I'll see tomorrow if it works.

Back in my room, I spend some time figuring out my next destination. Then, I call Kathy and tell her about my camping misadventures, the rain and my switch to "Plan B." That gets a nice laugh from Kathy. After updating my journal, I get in bed. Tomorrow, I plan to ride the Natchez Trace Trail

Sunday, August 31, 2003
Day Four: Arrive Natchez, Mississippi

It's 3:30AM and I'm wide awake. I force myself to lie in bed until 4AM, and then I get up. My packing is so much simpler without all that damn camping gear. I leave the camping stuff on the motel room floor with a note saying, "If you, motel people, can't use this stuff, call the Salvation Army or Good Will, they can use it." By 5AM, I'm on the road and right away, I hit heavy rain on I-10 West out of Mobile. Not only is it a hard rain with gusty winds, but it's still dark as hell. I've never ridden under these conditions. It is tough to see, especially with these 18-wheelers throwing up a blinding spray of dirty water in my face. On the bright side though, I have on my rain gear and I'm dry.

At 7:30AM, I stop for breakfast at an IHOP and call Kathy to let her know how I'm doing. I've been calling her about twice a day and I'm beginning to realize this cell phone has become an umbilical cord. But, Kathy likes to know how I'm doing and talk about her life at home. It's that and the fact that I never get tired of hearing her voice. After breakfast, more rain. I take off my rain gear as soon as I hit a clear spell; that stuff is hot. A few minutes later, more rain and I stop under an overpass to put it all back on again.

Around noon, I hit Route 61 and head north off I-10; this takes me to the start of the Natchez Trace Trail. The weather clears up again, so I stop and take off the rain gear. Surprise! A few minutes later, I run into a horde of love-bugs. They're coming at me like tracer bullets. It gets so bad I can only see the road by looking between the few tiny spaces on my face shield not yet covered with bug guts. Every time I pass a rest area I stop to wash the bugs off my face shield.

When I reach the town of Natchez at the beginning of the Natchez Trace Trail, it's about 2:30PM. I'm tired and hot. I realize I've been riding since 5AM. That's what, eight hours? No wonder I'm tired. It is too early to go to bed, but I'm done riding for today, so I stop at the Hatches Trace Visitor's Center and get a little info on tourist attractions. The best deal is the restored plantation-owner homes and slaves' quarters.

I turn around and go back a couple of miles to the last exit with motels. I spot one...The Executive Inn Motel. It is $38 per night with a

Sunday, August 31, 2003
Day Four: Arrive Natchez, Mississippi

laundry room, a little high for this place but it's still Labor Day weekend. I haul in my luggage, take a shower, and ride over to the Ruby Tuesday I spotted on the way into town for a late lunch. A tall, slender black girl, full of southern charm, serves my food and restores my energy even more than the tasty veggie burger and cold Heineken she serves me for lunch. With my new-found energy, I decide to take one of the plantation home tours. Taking guided tours is very unlike me, its Kathy's kind of thing and I always follow along, reluctantly. Nevertheless, it's just too early for bed and there's not much else to do.

It turns out, the tour is rather fascinating and I learn a few new things about plantations and slave life. For example, the guy that owned this mansion had five plantations, all of them were located far away from the mansion and he hired people to manage them. The slaves' quarters here were set up for one slave family per room. Right next to the owner's mansion stood the house-slaves quarters. They lived in small structures painted to look like an extension of the mansion. Outside slaves, the ones that did the gardening and cared for the grounds, lived in unpainted housing farther from the main house.

I read the book "Mandingo," a great book on slavery, published in the late fifties. I read it during the early '60s in the Navy. It described accounts of slaves being boiled in oil, tarred, and beaten with whips, along with tales of interracial sex between the beautiful female slaves and their white owners. In the mid-'70s, it became a movie starring James Mason. That decade also produced the TV docu-drama "Roots," which educated the whole country on slavery, but it was a little more sanitary than "Mandingo."

We still have a ways to go on racial issues, but we have made great progress. It took a hundred years after slavery was abolished for blacks to get civil rights laws passed and put an end to separate drinking fountains, separate toilet facilities, equal seating in restaurants and public transportation. Now the door of opportunity is open to all blacks. It's not entirely free of prejudice, but we are light years ahead of the slave era.

Sunday, August 31, 2003
Day Four: Arrive Natchez, Mississippi

When the tour is over, guess what? It starts raining again. Gee, what a surprise. Fortunately, after 20 minutes, it slows to a drizzle and I ride back to my motel to do my laundry. Now I am hungry again, so I ride back to Ruby Tuesdays and down another cold Heineken and another veggie burger with a side of steamed broccoli. Back in the motel, I update my journal and go to bed. Before falling asleep, I pray for just one day of dry weather

Monday, September 1, 2003
Day Five: Arrive Dumas, Arkansas

I'm up at 7:30AM. For breakfast, Shoney's is the only place I can find in Natchez. Man, this place has shitty food. On the way out, I'm paying my bill and the cashier asks, as they do so often, "How was everything?" Normally, I just say fine and leave, but I couldn't help myself this time, so I say, "You know, I can't think of another chain restaurant in America that has consistently worse food than Shoney's, it's really remarkably bad."

"Would you like to speak to the manager?" She asks. I think, 'Well, Pelton, this is your chance to straighten out Shoney's, so I say, "Yeah, why not?" A moment later, the kitchen doors swing open and a huge woman with an amiable smile strolls out and pleasantly introduces herself and asks if she can help me. I say, "Yes, your food is terrible."

"Can you be more specific?"

"Okay," I say, taking the challenge.

"Your breakfast buffet sucks. The peaches are sitting in a bowl of thick, murky syrup that looks and tastes terrible. The pancakes are hard around the edges and on top of all that, you don't serve oatmeal!"

"Is there anything else?" She politely asks. I think for a moment because I wasn't expecting her to ask that. Now I'm beginning to feel like this is a test and I better know the answers. "Yeah, okay, I have more. The rice tastes terrible too, I don't know what the hell it tastes like, but it's not like any rice I've ever tasted before and the home-fries are hard, like they were re-cooked a few times. They taste terrible."

"Is that all?" She asks.

"Jesus, isn't that enough? I can't believe you're asking me that question."

"Well, would you like to fill out a customer complaint form?"

"Hell no," I reply incredulously, "Why should I do work for your company? I'm telling you, that should be enough!" Now I am getting a little pissed and exasperated.

"Okay then," she says, maintaining a professionally polite attitude, "I'll pass on your suggestion about the oatmeal," she pauses. "But, I'll tell you the truth, I've worked here for ten years and no one

Monday, September 1, 2003
Day Five: Arrive Dumas, Arkansas

has ever complained about the food." I look around. Sure enough, everyone in the restaurant is busy stuffing their faces with Shoney's food and to my grudging surprise, they even seem happy. It's beyond my comprehension.

"Well, I guess I'm the only one," I say after scanning the customers. "Look, you seem like a very nice lady," I continue. "I just have a hard time believing your customers really like this food." I walk out shaking my head. How could I be so wrong about this? Am I the only person in 10 years that think their food sucks?

I have to oil my chain today. Where can I buy some chain oil? I also need to adjust the chain; it's too loose. So far, my big problem on this trip is it's either too wet, too hot or too many love-bugs. I need more good riding weather. After tightening my chain and buying some chain oil at an auto parts store, I'm on the road at 10AM. I feel content. I take the Natchez Trace Parkway north towards I-20. The Parkway was an old Indian trading route, eventually broadened and improved by white settlers in the early eighteen-hundreds. As I ride the trail, a narrow, two-lane road through dense forest and occasional clearings, I can imagine what a footpath or horse and wagon trail might have been like in those early times. I take off my riding jacket and casually ride the whole stretch in my T-shirt. The occasional light rain showers feel cool and refreshing because of the hot sun and high humidity. I cruise along at about 50 mph, occasionally stopping to absorb the scenery. Today is Labor Day, but it's also a Monday and the road is virtually empty. I guess all the tourists are headed home.

When I hit I-20, I head west. About 15 minutes later, I discover another good reason for wearing the motorcycle jacket currently strapped over my saddlebags: high-speed bugs. I get hit on the right arm by a couple of them. At 85 mph, they feel more like tiny high-speed stones. Then something stings my belly, again, and again, and again. "WHAT THE FUCK!" I hear myself shout. I strain to keep my composure, slow down and pull over on the shoulder of I-20. Jumping off the bike, I almost forget to put down my kickstand. As fast as

Monday, September 1, 2003
Day Five: Arrive Dumas, Arkansas

possible, I pull up my T-shirt and watch a swarm of bumblebees fly out in all directions leaving a dozen or so red welts all over my belly and chest.

Wait! It's still not over; something is stinging me inside my pants, in my pubic hairs. Oh shit, what's going on here? I unzip the fly on my jeans, pull them open and out tumbles one very confused bumblebee. Dazed at first, he quickly gets his bearings and flies away. Now I'm flapping my jeans to shake out any remaining bees. While surveying the damage to my torso and pubic region, it dawns on me…I'm standing on the side of a busy interstate, facing the traffic with my T-shirt pulled up under my chin, my pants down with my fly wide open and I'm not wearing any underwear. Some guy is probably driving by saying to his wife, "Hey, Susan, look at that idiot by the motorcycle. Is he flashing us?" I regain my composure, zip up my pants and thank my better angels for not having to explain this to a cop.

After this, I put my riding jacket back on. This feels better! The wind doesn't beat me around nearly as much. That wind can get pretty rough at highway speeds. I have a windscreen, but it's sloped-back and low, so it doesn't provide any protection to my upper body. Fortunately, the hundreds of tiny little ventilation holes in my jacket let in just enough fresh air to make me cool and still shield me from the harsher aspects of the environment. Now things are starting to go my way again.

Leaving I-20 West in Tallulah, Louisiana, I take route 65 North, a secondary highway that leads to Little Rock, Arkansas where I'll pick up on I-40 West. On Route 65, the quaint little towns tweak my emotions with abandoned stores and houses that stand as reminders of better days or, perhaps their time has just come and gone. Old-style southern homes with big front porches decorate the roadside. Many of them look like they could easily be the subject of a magazine pictorial on southern charm, or a Norman Rockwell painting. I'm coming upon a narrow river now, riding over the old two-lane bridge. To my right, is a huge old tree with leafy foliage extending over the shiny black river water. I see two boys with fishing poles sitting on the grassy bank,

Monday, September 1, 2003
Day Five: Arrive Dumas, Arkansas

waiting for a bite. I should stop and take a picture, but I just look instead. Images of Tom Sawyer and Huck Fin pop into my head.

 The people here are extremely polite. They always seem to have time for a little small-talk. Earlier today when I stopped for lunch at a Subway, a guy on the way to his car nodded hello, glanced at my license plate and asked me,

 "Comin' from Florida, huh?"

 "Yeah, I'm on a motorcycle vacation."

 "What's it like to ride in all this rain we've been getting lately?"

 "Makes me love the sunshine," I answered with a smile.

 "Well, you stay dry and have a nice trip, hear?"

 "Thanks, I will."

 A slower pace of life could do people in some parts of our country a lot of good. I did run into a little rain earlier today on Route 65, but it was more like sun-showers. Farther north on Route 65, it's mostly large spreads of farmland. As I cruise north, because the land is so flat, I can see the gray rainstorm formations to my left. They are not far away. They remind me of the gray storm formations I've seen far out in the ocean; they travel side by side but miles apart. Ominous looking things. I speed up to get on the other side of a big one before it crosses my path. A minute later, I look back and see it's crossing the highway just behind me. My good luck held for the whole day.

 The only dark spot today was when a big 18-wheeler passed me in the opposite direction and splashed muck all over my face shield, blinding me for a moment. I found it hard not to take the assault personally. At about 4PM, I decide to stop for the day. The last hour or so was tough on my back. The low handlebars mean most of my upper body weight is putting stress on my arms, but this gets better after a week or so of riding.

 I stop at the Executive Inn Motel in Dumas, Arkansas, a no-star motel for $32, right on Route 65. Big rooms. Space is cheap here in Dumas, but the amenities are sparse and crude: cheap fiberboard furniture, worn carpet, old sink and toilet facilities. After a shower, I find

Monday, September 1, 2003
Day Five: Arrive Dumas, Arkansas

a very forgettable Mexican restaurant nearby. The food is hot and filling, but they don't have a beer license and I have to drink water. I miss my two Heinekens.

While I'm eating, my mind travels back to this morning when I was having breakfast at Shoney's. This couple sitting at the table next to me, looking to be about 55 or so, saw my motorcycle from the window with the Florida plates and asked me,

"Are you traveling alone from Florida?"

"Yes, why do you ask?"

"Just curious. Do you enjoy traveling alone?"

"Yeah, I do actually," I answered. "I like it because I can travel at my own pace and do what I please when I want to do it. No compromises."

"Are you married?"

"Oh yeah, very happily," I answered with a friendly smile.

"Doesn't your wife like to ride with you?"

"Well," I said. "We've been married for 38 years. My wife used to ride with me, but she decided she had enough. She never got hurt and now she doesn't want to push her luck. I mean, we take vacations together, but the motorcycling is my thing."

Back at the motel, my daily call to Kathy leads to a conversation about Eddy's loose bowels and his diet. The positive side of that conversation is, other than Eddy's bowels, there are no problems at home I need to worry about

Tuesday, September 2, 2003
Day Six: Arrive Oklahoma City, Oklahoma

I say goodbye to Dumas at 8:20AM and head north to Little Rock; lots more farmland. The sky is threatening rain, nothing new about that. A few miles along, I ride past a little restaurant with a big sign that says, "Breakfast." Just what I need! A quick U-turn and I'm headed back. The place looks like a little country store and there is an old motor-home parked outside. I figure I'll have breakfast while Mother Earth decides if she wants to rain on me today. I order oatmeal, some fruit, potatoes and ketchup.

While I'm waiting for my order, I start a conversation with the older couple sitting at the next table. They tell me they're returning to Orlando in their motor-home after visiting their daughter and her family. Then the waitress, with a friendly face in her late 30s who's a bit on the plump side, delivers my order and jumps into the conversation.

"So, you're on a motorcycle trip, huh?"

"Yeah, from South Florida," I reply, "Down around Fort Lauderdale."

"My husband owns a motorcycle, a Shadow 1100," she says.

"Nice bike," I tell her.

"Yeah, we love it. We ride together every chance we get!"

I know the bike—it's a mid-sized cruiser. She hogs the conversation after that, telling me how much she and her husband like riding together and where they go. She is still running on about their Honda Shadow as I pay my bill at the checkout counter. Then, unbelievably, she follows me right out the door, still jabbering away. By this time, I'm glad to start up my bike and say goodbye. A few miles down the road, I realize I forgot to leave her a tip. I didn't feel bad enough to go back though.

A few minutes later, approaching Little Rock, I hit some light rain and stop to put on my two-piece rain suit. It is a smart move because when I reach I-40 heading west, the rain gets more intense. What the hell is it with all this rain? I manage to maintain my speed at 85 mph because there's no standing water and I'm able to see okay. At 4:30PM, I spot a Motel 6 at $35 a night in Oklahoma City and call it a day. It's hard to find cheesy

Tuesday, September 2, 2003
Day Six: Arrive Oklahoma City, Oklahoma

$19.95 motel rooms; maybe I'm looking in the wrong part of town. I found lots of them on my 1996 trip out west on the Harley.

I can't forget the time I checked into one rundown place at $17.95 a night. Right after I checked in, I was brushing my teeth over the sink in the bathroom. I leaned on the edge of the sink with my hand and the whole damn thing fell off the wall, crashing on the floor and breaking into a hundred pieces. I jumped back just in time, so it didn't hit my feet. I walked over to the office to tell the manager what happened, hoping he would not try to make me pay for the damage. He said, "Oh, I'm very sorry about that." Then he gave me the key to another room and said, "Let me know if you have any problems." I don't think he was too surprised.

Kathy is in a good mood when I call, staying busy and still concerned with Eddy's bowel movements; no worries at home. After my call to Kathy, I ride around the corner to a local tavern; it's a dingy, shotgun style interior with a bar about thirty-feet long on my right. In back of the bar are a few beer signs, scenic travel posters and some liquor bottles. On my left is just a bare wall. The lighting is dim and the front door is cocked open to let in some light and fresh air. I find an empty bar stool and order a Heineken. Some smart-ass down at the end of the bar says to the barmaid, "He just likes the sound of the name," implying I was a pretentious idiot. I want to shoot back with a sharp, smart-ass reply, but unfortunately, I can't think of one. So, I pretend like I don't hear him

Then the barmaid tells me, "We don't have any Heineken." I look around and I see everyone is drinking Bud and Bud Lite. Now I know where the guy at the end of the bar was coming from, but I'm still not interested in a Bud. I look again and see they have Tecate, a pretty good Mexican beer, so I order that.

The guy sitting one bar stool to my left looks about my age. I find out he's a real motorcycle nut. Used to race dirt bikes and still owns several vintage Yamahas and a few others. We bullshit about motorcycles for almost an hour. The barmaid, Julie, joins our

Tuesday, September 2, 2003
Day Six: Arrive Oklahoma City, Oklahoma

conversation in between handling customers, not to talk about bikes though; she wants to know where I'm from and where I'm going. Julie looks like she's in her late thirties, maybe five-foot-eight and pretty with dirty blonde hair.

Two empty bar stools to my right is an old guy. I swear to god, he looks very close to dead, bent over staring into his glass of beer. Julie comes around to our side of the bar and starts kidding around with this old guy because she knows him, "He's been coming here just about forever," she tells me.

As she says this, the old guy grins and comes to life. He sits up and turns around on his bar stool, looking at Julie. "Jack is a horny old goat," Julie says, smiling my way, "aren't you, Jack?" Jack answers by reaching out with both hands, wiggling all his fingers like he wants to feel her tits. So, Julie takes his hands and places them on her breasts and wiggles her ass to give old Jack a charge.

"He's 82 and harmless," she says with a smile, looking at me and the motorcycle guy I'm talking with. Then she adds, "He deserves this. But, if anyone else tries it on me, I'll deck him." Now I'm thinking, there is at least one benefit to getting old in Oklahoma City, thanks to good-natured Julie. Between Julie and the motorcycle guy, I get a lead to an excellent Italian restaurant over in what's known as "Brick Town."

So, after a hot shower, I ride over to find this restaurant. Brick Town is the original downtown Oklahoma City. Everything, of course, is old brick. The central section of Brick Town is on two levels with a narrow canal running through the center. Ground level is mostly shops and a few restaurants, teeming with people walking in and out of the shops or just strolling on the sidewalk that runs along the canal. It's very charming and romantic at night with simulated gas lanterns in front of the little shops and along the canal.

On the upper level are restaurants with elaborate patios that overlook the canal. Water taxies glide back and forth filled with people that seem to love the place for its atmosphere and excellent dining. If

Tuesday, September 2, 2003
Day Six: Arrive Oklahoma City, Oklahoma

you have ever been to The River Walk in San Antonio, Texas, you'll know what this place is like; it's patterned after San Antonio.

I try the Italian place that Julie recommended, but it doesn't appeal to me, so I walk across the upper-level footbridge to the other side of the canal and decide to eat at Chelino's, a Mexican restaurant. The weather now is beautiful, so I pick a small, outdoor patio table and order a burrito stuffed with veggies and no cheese. Not surprisingly, they got it right except for the cheese part. The waitress was friendly though and takes it back. A few minutes later, I have a hot burrito with no cheese and another ice-cold Tecate. It tastes outstanding. When the waitress brings my check, I smile…it's only $10.93. Amazing!

Riding back to my motel, I pay close attention to my front brakes; they are chattering when I stop at low speed, Worn brake pads? Uneven discs? I've noticed it since I left home, but now it's getting worse. Why didn't they see this when I had the bike prepped at the Honda place? I don't like riding it like this. I make a mental note to drive by a Honda motorcycle dealer tomorrow and let them take a look at it.

Wednesday, September 3, 2003
Day Seven: Arrive Tucumcari, New Mexico

Leaving Motel 6 in Oklahoma City at 8AM, I continue west on I-40. Twenty minutes into the ride, I see a heavy overcast in the foreground. I can't figure out what it is. It looks like rain, but not quite. A mile later, I find out. It's fog. Immediately, my face shield fogs up so I can barely see the road. I slow down and flip up my face shield to look through my glasses. An 18-wheeler roars past me because I'm going too slow. Now my glasses are fogging up. I can barely see anything. Intimidated by the traffic whizzing by, I pull over and wipe the moisture from my face shield and eyeglasses with a rag from my tank bag. Five minutes later, I'm doing the same thing again. I have little experience riding in fog and on a busy interstate with virtually no vision, it's scary.

After a couple of stops, I discover that if I lie forward with my chest on the tank bag and lower my head behind my windscreen just right, the wind coming off the top edge of the sweptback, windscreen will blow the condensation off my face-shield. Now, I can see fairly well. My fears dissipate. Soon, the fog clears. Now the weather is cool and crisp, like a beautiful fall day. I stop to put on my jacket-liner because even modestly cool weather turns downright cold at highway speeds due to ventilation holes in my jacket and the wind chill factor. Now that I'm warm, I couldn't ask for more beautiful riding conditions.

Old Route 66 follows parts of I-40. As I enter Elk City, Oklahoma, I see a billboard advertising National Route 66 Museum. I have to check this out, so I stop. The place is filled with auto-related nostalgia from the 1930s, '40s and '50s: old cars, early gas station relics and big wall-photo murals of Route 66 stores, motels and families traveling in old Buicks and Studebakers. I was born in 1942, so I recall much of this. Things looked a lot different back then, a lot less complicated for sure.

Leaving Elk City, I don't see a Honda dealer, but I do spot a Kawasaki-Suzuki dealer. I stop in and ask him to take a look at my front brakes. He bends down, takes a quick look and confirms my brake pads are shot. "I don't carry those pads but you can get them at the Honda dealer just off I-40 as you enter Amarillo, you'll see it on the right just as you enter the town."

Wednesday, September 3, 2003
Day Seven: Arrive Tucumcari, New Mexico

"What do I owe you?"

"Nothing," he tells me. "I didn't fix anything."

"Well, thank you very much then." Amarillo, Texas is 250 miles from here with nothing but flat ranch and farmland along I-40. It's a good road for riding fast. I find the Honda dealer with no problem and after a 90-minute wait, I'm back on the road with new front brakes. What a difference, the bike stops like it hit super-glue and the stops are smooth too. That was a quick $140, but the new brakes get me thinking about what happened yesterday on I-40 when I had to make an emergency stop to avoid hitting a dog.

Traffic was heavy and very fast when I spotted a medium-sized black dog crossing the interstate. Incredibly, the dog made it across both the busy east and westbound lanes, a small miracle in itself. Unknown to me, he was waiting for his friend stuck on the grassy median strip to finish his crossing and join him. I was cruising in the fast lane next to the median strip when I spotted the second dog. He makes a run for it and then, out of fear, he stops dead, right in my lane. I can see he's scared stiff and doesn't know what to do next. I hit both front and back brakes hard. The cars in the two lanes to my right only slow down a bit. I only had two things on my mind: one, that my front or rear wheel wouldn't lock up as I have no ABS; and two, that the guy behind me was also stopping on time.

Fast approaching the dog, I was slowed to under 20 mph when it scampered back to the median strip. Then, before I could even think anymore about the dog, I downshifted and took off again, fearing someone would smash into me from the rear. There was no room to pull over by the grassy median strip. By the time I raced ahead of the cars in the two lanes to my right and parked on the edge of the road, I'd be at least a half-mile away and maybe much more. A U-turn was not in sight.

I feel guilty and ashamed of myself for not doing something. Why didn't I stop? Simple inconvenience? I've been replaying that guilt-ladened dog incident in my mind since yesterday and I know it will haunt me for a long time to come.

Wednesday, September 3, 2003
Day Seven: Arrive Tucumcari, New Mexico

I stop at a Denny's in Amarillo, Texas for lunch before continuing west to New Mexico on I-40. Here, like much of I-40 elsewhere, the scenery is uninteresting. It's primarily rural farmland. However, after leaving Amarillo, I do see a huge white Christian cross that must have been 200 feet tall, and close to that was an old water tower that looked like it was about to fall over. About an hour later, not long after I cross the New Mexico state line, I see a blue flashing light in my rearview mirror. I pull over.

The highway patrol car stops just behind me. We exchange pleasantries. I give him my license and he asks me if I know how fast I was going. I plead ignorance. So, he tells me I was going 87 mph, 12 mph over the 75 mph limit. "I'm going to ticket you for going 85, 10 mph over the posted limit," he says. "It will cost you less, only 65 dollars, and it will help with your car insurance."

"Thanks," I tell him and wonder, why is it I'm always thanking cops for giving me a ticket? A ticket for going 87 mph, how uninteresting. Getting ticketed for doing 130 would be much more exciting, but a lot more expensive too. Still, it's another $65 on top of the one $140 brake job this morning.

A few minutes later, I enter Tucumcari, New Mexico. It's about 5PM and I feel fatigued. I see The Pony Soldier Motel for $19.95. All right! A cheap, sleaze-bag motel, just what I'm looking for. I check-in for the night. The beat-up old car parked next to my motorcycle is covered with dust from the gravel parking lot and it has a flat front tire. The tires also have watermarks from the rising mud of the parking lot during prior rainfalls. It was easy to tell it had been parked here for a long time. Maybe the owner ran out of money and left it.

The room is clean…one bed, a beat-up, nineteen-inch TV set on top of a cheap, wood-veneer dresser and a basic, white porcelain sink sticking out of the wall near the shower and toilet. I open the bent Venetian blinds to let in some light and unload my luggage on the threadbare carpet.

Wednesday, September 3, 2003
Day Seven: Arrive Tucumcari, New Mexico

After washing my hands and splashing some cold water on my face, I leave to find a cold brew. On Old Route 66 I spot a bar. The parking lot outside has nothing but pickup trucks. I count them, there are eight. All of them are muddy and dented and parked side by side. No cars. I park close to the front door and walk in. The lighting is low. Two very well-used pool tables are on my right and the bar, maybe 28 feet long, is on my left. Two old cowboy types are shooting pool at one table, and two younger men play at the other table. The "old boys" are dressed in worn jeans, old cowboy shirts, hats and muddy, scuffed-up cowboy boots. The two younger guys are dressed in jeans, sneakers and baseball caps.

I'm the only tourist in the joint. After I order a beer, I strike up a conversation with the old cowboy sitting next to me. He looks to be in his mid-70s. He asks where I came from, which I explain and I ask him if he has roots in the area. "My father," he says plainly, "came to New Mexico in 1902. He was a rancher. He raised me here until I got a bug up my ass and left in 1942." He takes a pause to sip his beer and says, "But I came back here to live for good in '52." He tells me he's seventy-eight and it's easy for me to see he's proud of his New Mexico heritage. After two beers, I feel like riding back to my motel and cleaning up. A warm shower restores my energy. I put on a fresh black T-shirt, a clean pair of jeans and return to the same bar.

Now there are two black Harleys parked outside the bar. The same regulars are here and two new customers are drinking at the bar. They look like Harley riders with black leather vests, boots, and jeans. I assume they're on the two bikes parked outside, probably touring the area. I take the open seat next to them. One of the two bikers is a female, probably in her early 50s. Her face has a slightly weathered look. However, she has a trim body and her facial features show a classically beautiful bone structure. She must have been quite a beauty in her youth. The guy looks to be in his early forties and handsome in a rugged way with a lean, rangy body on the tall side, maybe six-foot-two.

Wednesday, September 3, 2003
Day Seven: Arrive Tucumcari, New Mexico

They're quietly engrossed in each other, I suspect, talking about their travels. I can't really follow their conversation, but I detect an unusual accent, maybe Australian. During a pause, I ask them if the two Harleys outside belong to them. They answer "Yes," and the woman says they are touring the country.

"I'm on a motorcycle vacation too," I tell them, from South Florida. "You two sound like you may be from Australia," I ask, uncertainly. The woman answers, "No, we're both Kiwis, you know, from New Zealand," she glances at her companion who nods his head in affirmation.

"Oh, I'm sorry," I say, a little embarrassed that I couldn't pick up on their accent. "So you're touring the country together?" I ask innocently, expecting another affirmative response.

"Actually," the guy says, "we never laid eyes on each other until we met in this bar about an hour ago."

"You've got to be kidding!" I say, astonished.

"No, it's true," the woman replies. "We just met."

The guy tells me he's been touring the U.S. for six weeks and was on his way to Los Angeles to fly home. The woman says she started her travels in early July and will be going back home in late September.

"How do you take trips so far away from home and for so long a time?" I ask.

"Well it's not that simple," the guy tells me. "When I told my employer how long I'd be gone, he told me I may have to look for other employment when I get home.

"Because he can't hold your job open?" I ask.

"Yeah, that's right."

The woman tells me she saved almost every penny she earned for two and a half years to do this trip and she had to quit her job. She isn't sure what she'll do when she gets home.

People like this fascinate me. They go on these big adventures and risk life-changing consequences with their careers, not to mention the risks of traveling by motorcycle in a strange country for months all

Wednesday, September 3, 2003
Day Seven: Arrive Tucumcari, New Mexico

alone. I think everyone has a real adventure fantasy at one time or another. Most people never act on them. Why not? Well, money, fear, family responsibilities, jobs, you name it. But some people just say, fuck it! They go for it and live with the consequences. Anyway, these two people from the same far away country were undoubtedly living their dream adventure and strangely meet each other at this nowhere bar in a poor little New Mexico town called Tucumcari. Pretty weird, even poetic.

My conversation with the two "Kiwis" winds down and my attention drifts to the guy playing pool in back of my barstool a few feet away. This old cowboy has been beating all his challengers for the last hour or more. He's good. While pausing to take a sip from his Bud while his opponent makes a shot, I jokingly ask, "Hey, how do you do that… I mean, how come you never lose?"

"Because I don't give a shit," he answers with a cocky grin. He wins the game and voluntarily gives up control of the table to his challenger, then he takes a seat at the bar next to me with his beer. He says "Really, the reason I win is that I don't a give a shit about winning… or losing." Then he explains
his philosophy further by adding, "If you care too much, you can't win."

His worn cowboy garb, weathered face and quiet confidence give him the aura of an old philosopher. He's probably about my age, 60 or so, but looks older; he clearly spends a lot of time outdoors. He tells me his name is Bill. He seems like a friendly sort, so we continue talking. From his general drift, I can tell he has a liberal, live and let live, attitude on life. We touch on the war in Iraq. He says he was against the war from the start and he thinks Bush is an asshole. I shake my head in agreement

This leads to a discussion about Republicans and the religious right which leads to a conversation about religion in general. He tells me, "I gave up on all religions a long time ago. That doesn't mean I don't believe in God. I just don't like religion; it's got everything to do with other people telling me what to think and very little about God."

Wednesday, September 3, 2003
Day Seven: Arrive Tucumcari, New Mexico

"I can understand that," I tell him, taking a sip of beer. "I feel the same way." Then we move on to paranormal and metaphysical subjects and I find out he is well read in that area too.

"Yeah, I don't doubt some of those UFO's are real and I've heard of that guy Edgar Casey, he's the guy that used to put himself in a trance and diagnose sick people, the ones the doctors had given up on."

Finally, when the conversation gets back to politics and the war, I realize we had just about gone full circle with our barstool conversation. Somehow, the subject of food comes up and I honestly tell Bill I don't eat animal products. That changes the tone of the conversation entirely. He gets quieter after that and I can tell his attitude is changing. He excuses himself to go to the men's room. When he comes back, he confesses, "I have a little problem with that vegetarian stuff."

Right then, I know I shouldn't be talking to old cowboys in New Mexico about my discipline of not eating animals. Bill was brought up eating meat and raising cattle. We chat a bit more, but the conversation is a little strained. So, realizing I better go eat before the restaurant's closed, I down the rest of my beer and bid my bar-mate farewell. The first place I spot is a Denny's, the second time today. I order the same thing, a veggie burger, hash browns and a garden salad. Not bad. With nothing else to do while I wait for my order, I watch my waitress. I wonder if she is still in high school because she looks very young, so I ask her.

"Oh no, I'm 21. I've been out of school for a long time," she answers with a friendly smile. She's very sharp. You know how sometimes you can just sense this in people? As I eat, with nothing else to do, I watch the way she handles taking care of the customers. She is efficient, attentive, polite and clearly overqualified for her Denny's waitress job. When she comes back to give me my check, I say, "I was watching you work, you're terrific and clearly overqualified for this job."

She smiles and says, "Oh, thank you."

Wednesday, September 3, 2003
Day Seven: Arrive Tucumcari, New Mexico

"You can have a bright future; you have what it takes, I can see it."
She looks at me like she genuinely wants to believe what I am saying and tells me, "Gee, I really hope so. Thank you very much. You made me feel a lot better about myself. I'll try." I guess she means she'll try to make something of herself beyond being a Denny's waitress. I hope so; she's a sharp kid.

As I'm riding back to my motel, I wonder again about the two Kiwis I met earlier at the bar. They both love traveling alone by motorcycle. It's an exciting way to travel, but you have to deal with lots of adversities, like extreme weather, mechanical problems, fatigue and more. Why do people do this?

Motorcycling is a mode of travel directly connected to the environment like the cowboys and their horses of a bygone era, and it still captures our imagination. When you ride a horse, you feel the raw power of the horse between your legs and the force of the wind on your face and body. There's a real sense of freedom and excitement, so it is with a motorcycle. We all know how breathtaking a wild horse looks rearing up on its back legs, compelling us to look and appreciate its wild beauty, strength and sense of unbridled freedom. Motorcycles have a similar essence. A well-controlled wheelie is one of the most dangerous and challenging motorcycle stunts to pull off, but few feats give the rider a bigger rush or compel more awe from onlookers. Watch a motorcyclist loft his bike's front wheel high into the air at 60 mph; it's a stunning sight.

For a motorcyclist, the trip is the destination. When you're riding, you are living in the present moment. Experiencing the real-world environment is an integral part of the whole thing. It's only by enduring, firsthand, the adversity of a harsh and scary thunderstorm in the morning that you can appreciate the full beauty and delight of a sunny, dry afternoon. The yin and yang. It's the key to staying in touch with nature and living every moment of the journey. That's what makes it an experience that causes people to dream about getting on their bike

Wednesday, September 3, 2003
Day Seven: Arrive Tucumcari, New Mexico

and traveling to faraway places. You can't have a real adventure without adversity.

Tucumcari is an unfortunate place. I noticed this earlier, while I was riding around looking for a place to have a beer. It's located on Route 66, which merges off and on with I-40. It's about three miles long with a population of maybe 15,000. The town is dotted with rows of three, four and five buildings standing vacant—victims of the Interstate and changing demographics. Some look like they've been abandoned for years. I see this throughout the town. The original downtown area is like a ghost town. There's an old movie theater from the fifties in poor repair. Many of the stores are closed up for good, and the buildings look abandoned and run down; it's kind of a dismal place to live. It's no wonder I got a motel for $19.95 a night

Thursday, September 4, 2003
Day Eight: Arrive Gallup, New Mexico

I'm on the road early this morning, about 7:30AM. I'm not sure which path I'll take today. I have two choices: I-40 West to Albuquerque or Route104northwest to Las Vegas, New Mexico, then back to Albuquerque on a scenic backroad called the Turquoise Trail. I hate riding on the interstate; it's monotonous. The only fun thing to do is speed and pass cars and, as I found out yesterday, that can get expensive.

It's a beautiful morning, crisp and bright; no fog, thank God. I hate fog. The bike feels good too, the engine sounds tight and responds eagerly to the throttle. I got a good night's sleep and feel refreshed, ready for an enjoyable day of riding. I decide to take 104 northwest to Las Vegas, New Mexico and have breakfast there. I'm interested to know what it's all about and why it's called Las Vegas. I have no idea what Route 104 is like, but it has to be a pleasant departure from the interstate.

I'm not disappointed; the scenery is beautiful. I see high plateaus off in the distance and on both sides of the narrow, two-lane road are huge ranches and pastureland with grazing herds of cattle. Looking more carefully, I notice the steers are on my left and the cows on my right. I pass by a lone black bull on the left side of the road with his horns and snout pressed against the wire-mesh fence. He is bellowing through the fence to a small group of cows on my right. He's trying to entice them over to his side, but the females are not impressed.

Some ranchers have constructed beautiful, two-story homes with great, columned front-entrances sitting on expansive well-manicured lawns. In between these impressive homes, it's common to see stretches of smaller ranch-style houses, many with old cars and trucks rusting away on their property. Some of the ranch-style dwellings are dilapidated beyond repair. The people have moved into a mobile home that now sits next to the old house. I see a few, lots with one dilapidated house and three relatively new mobile homes nearby. Of course, the requisite rusty old cars and trucks are there too. The entire transportation and housing history of these families is right here to see.

It appears that when the family house finally becomes unlivable, they move out to the mobile home and maybe buy one for the grown

Thursday, September 4, 2003
Day Eight: Arrive Gallup, New Mexico

children too. The same with old cars and trucks. The old stuff never leaves the yard. They just buy something newer, never know if you'll need replacement parts, why get rid of the old stuff? And besides, where are they going to take it? It may be a hundred miles to the nearest junkyard.

At 8AM, I notice a sign that says altitude 6,300 feet. No wonder I'm getting colder by the minute. I stop and put on my jacket liner. That's much better. It's about 10AM when I reach an elevation of 8,000 feet and pull into Las Vegas. This is a clean, bustling little town high up in the middle of nowhere. I stop for breakfast at a Mexican restaurant which I think is a little strange because this is the first Mexican restaurant I've ever seen in the United States that serves breakfast. Inside, it's quite clean and must be a favorite eating place because it's bustling with customers.

It appears, all the staff is Mexican. Fortunately, for me, they speak English very well. Now I can find out what Mexicans eat for breakfast. It turns out they eat eggs and meat, just like Americans. Oh good, they also have oatmeal, home-fries, fruit and coffee, so I order that. I get out my cell-phone while I'm waiting for my check and call my old friend Tony. Not visiting anyone was a rule on this trip but Tony moved to Las Vegas, Nevada three months ago from South Florida and I promised to visit him and see his new house. He also likes to play poker in the casinos and wants to take me with him to play. He's expecting me any day now so he won't be surprised to hear from me.

Tony answers the phone and after we exchange greetings, I say, "Hey Tony, I'm getting pretty close to your place."

"Really, where are you?" He sounds happy and eager to see me.

"Well, I'm in Las Vegas," I answer.

"No shit, where? I'll come over and get you."

Then I tell him "Las Vegas, New Mexico." There's a long pause while the gears in his brain turn over, then I hear a big laugh.

Walking around the small, town center, I see the chamber of commerce is right next to the restaurant where I ate breakfast. So, I stop

Thursday, September 4, 2003
Day Eight: Arrive Gallup, New Mexico

in and ask the receptionist about the town. The lady explains that the town sprung up from the early Santa Fe Trail travelers. This was the first place on the long trail that had any drinkable water so everyone would stop here to refresh themselves and their animals.

Entrepreneurs soon got the idea of selling other goods and services to the weary travelers and before long, the merchants settled here and it became a thriving town. The town still looks like it's doing okay too, with lots of well-kept stores and small office buildings. Tourism looks good. On the way in, I saw several motorcyclists with touring gear riding through town. The chamber lady gives me directions to the Turquoise Trail, which is about fifty miles long. It's the back road between Albuquerque and Santa Fe. The Spanish explorer, Francisco Vasquez de Coronado was the first white man to use the trail in the early 1500s. This territory was still part of Mexico back then. Later, frontiersmen like Kit Carson, along with thousands of new settlers, used the Trail until it became a regular road.

The trail area contains what is probably the oldest mine in North America—a turquoise mine first worked on by Indians going back to 1000 B.C.E., and later by Spanish, Mexican and American miners. Hence the name, Turquoise Trail. They also mined coal from these hills for a while, but it was stopped and didn't have a lasting impact on the area's beauty. I rode the scenic trail on my Harley when I was out here in '95 and want to see it again. Eccentric painters, artisans and people that enjoy a secluded lifestyle populate the trail. Most of them specialize in making turquoise jewelry and related artwork, then they sell it in the small shops along the trail and wherever else they can find a market.

Just outside of Las Vegas, I catch I-25 South for a short way and head for Route 14, which is also a part of the Turquoise Trail. The roads on the trail are very narrow and twisty. You never know what will appear in front of you as these curves unfold, so I'm careful. I don't want panic breaking on these curves with sharp drop-offs of one thousand feet or more. The weather is still clear. It is a beautiful day for motorcycling. About noontime, I come to a small village at the halfway

Thursday, September 4, 2003
Day Eight: Arrive Gallup, New Mexico

point to Albuquerque. I stop, mainly to stretch my legs and get a cool drink. The most attractive place for food or a beer is a large, rustic looking saloon.

Two BMW touring bikes packed with traveling gear are parked outside. Inside, the place has an authentic old-west look, but about half the customers are tourists, so that takes something away. The menu doesn't have anything I care for, but I'm not hungry anyway. I had a substantial breakfast, so I order a bottle of Bass Ale from the ample beer menu and strike up a conversation with the guy on the barstool to my left. He's a local guy in his late 40s. I ask him what he does here to make a living. He tells me he's a "jack-of-all-trades" and has lived on the trail since 1972.

After a little small talk, he tells me he's moving to Richmond, Virginia to marry a girl he's been going with for 30 years. He's had a lot of other relationships in the 30 years but keeps going back to this woman; now he's going to marry her. I wish him luck, thinking to myself, 'he'll need it.' He just doesn't strike me as the kind of guy that can make up his mind.

My ride on the Turquoise Trail ends back on I-40 at about 1PM, and I continue to head west. I want to do another 130 miles to reach Gallup, New Mexico…about halfway between Albuquerque and Flagstaff, Arizona. It's unusual to get a whole day without rain, so I'm not surprised when the weather
turns wet about halfway to Gallup, no hard rain, just lots of drizzle. I can see massive storms and lightning to the north, but it doesn't look like it's headed my way.

Later in the afternoon, however, as the sun recedes into the horizon, the cold air blowing down the back of my jacket cuts right to my bones. This causes the muscles in my back and neck to tighten up like a clenched fist. Finally, I give in and put on my jacket-liner and two-piece rain-suit. I feel warmer now. I'm getting tired though because I've been riding since 7:30AM and now it's 4 o'clock. I'm ready to call it a day.

Thursday, September 4, 2003
Day Eight: Arrive Gallup, New Mexico

I make the 130 miles to Gallup and check into the El Capitan Motel for $25. After my daily call to Kathy, I realize I'm starving because I haven't eaten since 10AM. The little Mexican restaurant across the street is perfect. I write in my journal while sipping on an ice-cold Heineken, then enjoy my second one while I hungrily devour a large veggie-bean burrito. Delicious! After filling my belly with beer and hot food, I head back to my motel, take a hot shower, write more in my journal and quickly fall asleep. It was a good day.

After two hours of sleep, I wake up with a start. Christ, all my clothes are dirty! I really don't feel like doing this, but I sort out all my dirty laundry and spend the next two hours at the laundromat.

Friday, September 5, 2003
Day Nine: Arrive Fredonia, Arizona

After a good breakfast and a lot of vacillation, I decide not to take I-40 directly to Las Vegas, Nevada. Instead, I'll take Route 264, a two-lane road that goes north into the Painted Desert, through some mountains near the north entrance to the Grand Canyon and then circles back south to Las Vegas on I-15. Actually, it's Route 264 to Route 89 alternate to Route 389 to I-15 South. The weather is beautiful and the Painted Desert is incredible, even though Kathy and I have seen it before. Lots of red earth shaped into majestic formations. Wide open, flat plains, cattle ranches with long, beautiful, red plateaus in the background. And, every now and then, large patches of uniformly short, round-topped trees. Small settlements dot the landscape along the highway. They're mostly ranch-style homes, just basic structures with lots of mobile homes thrown in. The whole area is Hopi Indian country. It's their land.

My testicles have been driving me crazy for the last two days, especially toward the end of the day. They have a way of getting squished between me and the gas tank. I stop to buy gas at a general store in the middle of nowhere and go inside to stretch my legs and look around. I spot a small Indian blanket for ten dollars. Maybe this will help mitigate my squished testicle problem. For 10 bucks, I'll take a chance. Back outside, I fold it into a big square and lay it on my seat. Then I secure it with a nylon strap that I run under and over the seat.

My next problem is cold air blowing down the back of my neck. During the last few days, it has developed something like a cold in my muscle tissue around my upper back and between my shoulder blades. Once again, it occurs mostly in the afternoon when fatigue sets in. To cure this problem, I take the small towel I use to wipe the moisture off my seat in the morning and wrap it around my neck like a scarf. Back on the road, I feel great.

By 4PM, I'm in Fredonia, Arizona and I'm tired. Since the towns are far apart up here, I decide to call it a day. Fredonia is a small tourist stop for visitors headed to the north rim of the Grand Canyon. I find a motel, the only one in town. It's called the Crazy Jug Motel. It's 35 bucks a night, not bad for the only place in town.

Friday, September 5, 2003
Day Nine: Arrive Fredonia, Arizona

After unloading my saddlebags, I try calling Kathy on my cellphone. No luck, the area is too remote. The hotel manager tells me there's a pay phone a quarter-mile up the street. I try that, three minutes for 25 cents. It's enough time to tell Kathy I'm still alive. The only problem, Kathy's not home. Shit! I leave a message on our recorder, telling her I'm okay. Then, I ride back to the motel to wash up a bit before riding four miles to the opposite end of town to have a beer at the only bar in town.

I spot the bar on my left. It has a large, parking area covered with big round stones. It feels like I'm riding on marbles. I'm glad I don't have my luggage on the bike. The problem with riding on stones at low speed isn't the tires moving and slipping. The problem occurs when the bike comes to a stop and I put my feet on the ground to steady the bike. If I'm not careful, my foot will slip on the loose stones and surprise, I've got 500 pounds of motorcycle lying on the ground. That's a lot of motorcycle for a 150-pound guy to pick up. More importantly, it's very embarrassing.

I successfully park the bike and slip a flat rock, about six inches across, under the kickstand so it won't slip between the round stones and sink into the soft sand. Inside, I order a Heineken and say hello to the crusty looking old guy sitting on the bar stool to my left. After our pleasantries, I ask him, while pointing to the pack of short, unfiltered Camels lying on the bar, "Do you smoke these? I didn't know you could even buy these anymore because all I ever see are the king-size, filtered Camels."

"Oh yeah, they're mine," he says, and goes on to say, "I've been smoking them since I was 15...I'm 75 now." He says this with a bit of pride. "So, I guess I kind of beat the odds."

After a bit of small talk about the town, where I'm from and my motorcycle vacation, he goes on to tell me more about himself.

He says he's been retired for quite a while now and that he grew up in Wyoming. "I've been a truck driver all my life," he says. "My daddy taught me how to drive on his pickup when I was 13. Later, I

Friday, September 5, 2003
Day Nine: Arrive Fredonia, Arizona

graduated to 18-wheelers…tankers mostly, and I've been driving trucks ever since." He says he drove for the big oil companies like Shell and Exxon.

    I ask him if he ever had an accident. "No, not really." He says in between taking a drag of a short camel and a sip of Bud. Then, I ask him if he ever had one jack-knife on him. "Yeah, only one time. I was coming over the crest of a hill in the snow and a flock of sheep had parked themselves in the middle of the road. I hit the brakes and the rig jack-knifed. But it wasn't my fault and the company didn't give me any trouble over it."

    He confesses he did lose his driver's license later in life due to a DWI arrest. He says he spent 13 days in jail, during which time he wasn't allowed to smoke. "When I got out, I stayed off cigarettes for two more weeks," he tells me with feigned pride. "But then I took up drinkin' again and started back smoking. I haven't quit since and to tell you the truth, I've never regretted it. I have to spend about 10 minutes every morning hackin' up phlegm, but after that, I'm okay for the day."

    About the time he finishes telling me his stories, I take the last swallow of my second beer and bid goodbye to the old guy. Now I'm getting hungry and want to find a restaurant. Outside, I mount my bike and head back to my motel looking for a restaurant on the way. I spot one, but it is still under construction. Fortunately, my motel has a restaurant. This is a strange place: one bar, one restaurant and one motel. Kind of reminds me of the proverbial, "one-horse town."

    I'm surprised to see two veggie entrees on the menu and I order them both: a veggie burger and a veggie wrap, plus a big salad. I'm starving. I wash it down with a non-alcoholic beer. While I'm eating, I'm mulling over tomorrow's ride. I decide making it to Tony's house in Las Vegas early in the day should be a piece of cake because it's mostly interstate all the way once I get on I-15. After dinner, I call Kathy again from the pay phone. She sounds good and tells me everything is okay on her end. Finally, after a hot shower, I catch up on my journal entries and fall asleep

Saturday, September 6, 2003
Day Ten: Arrive Los Vegas, Nevada

A loud, driving thunderstorm wakes me from a pleasant sleep. It's 7:30AM, time to get up anyway so there's nothing lost. By the time I'm dressed, the rain lets up and I walk across the expansive, white-pebble covered parking lot for some oatmeal, hash-browns and coffee at the only restaurant in town. After breakfast, I pack my luggage and wipe the bike's seat dry. The weather has turned clear and crisp. Being back on the bike is good.

It's one of those special mornings just made for motorcycling. With my cold weather, jacket-liner under my motorcycle jacket, the cool morning air is just enough to invigorate my senses. The morning sun is breaking out; sweet. Even the grass and shrubs alongside the road look happy and sparkle with water drops from the early morning thunderstorm—a beautiful sight. I'm on Route 389, a two-lane road with very little traffic, and I own the road for the next 60 miles until I hit the entrance to the interstate. Just before getting onto I-15, I gas up for the 150-mile run into Las Vegas. From where I am, a little north of St. George, Utah, I-15 heads southwest, cutting across the northwest tip of Arizona and then on into Nevada.

Entering Nevada on I-15 has got to be one of the most impressive and beautiful strips of interstate in the country. It winds through magnificent multi-colored mountain passes with long sweeping turns, uphill, downhill, through a quarter-mile long tunnel. It's a truly delightful ride. The shiny black asphalt is wide with an expansive and sweeping vista of the desert. I cruise at 100 mph and soon enter a long curve around the upper perimeter of a peak. I whiz past a string of four cars before heading into a big, downhill sweeper. From this elevation, I can appreciate the natural beauty for as far as my eyes can see. I flash by a Harley rider. He's relaxed, his bike loaded with luggage. I wonder if he's having as much fun as I am.

Nothing lasts forever of course, and as I get closer to sea level, I-15 straightens out and the fun is over. Now, at the lower altitude, the sun is very bright and it's getting quite warm. I pull over on the ample shoulder, stretch my legs and take off my cold weather jacket-liner. While I'm stuffing my jacket-liner back into my luggage, the guy on the

Saturday, September 6, 2003
Day Ten: Arrive Los Vegas, Nevada

Harley cruises by and we wave at each other. A few miles down the road, I pass him again; it's like the tortoise and the hare. I'm getting close to Las Vegas now and the heat is getting oppressive. The traffic is getting thicker too and now I can see the tall buildings along the strip.

Before I get lost, I better stop and call Tony for directions. On my cell-phone, I describe where I am and Tony tells me I'm very close to his house. He gives me directions and I scribble them on my notepad under his phone number. I'm a little annoyed now because I expected him to meet me near town and lead me to his house. Without thinking, I immediately head in the wrong direction. It takes me 10 minutes to realize my mistake. Now I'm hot, I'm lost and I'm getting pissed at Tony. He gives me these stupid directions, I think because he's too fucking lazy to come and meet me. This isn't good, I haven't even said hello to Tony and I'm already pissed at him. I decide to get a grip on myself and give him the benefit of the doubt.

After re-reading his directions, I try again. This time, I go right to his house. Actually, his directions were perfect, I just didn't follow them on the first try because they didn't seem to make sense. At the door, Tony and his wife, Marion, both greet me with a warm hug and kiss. The kiss between men is very old-world Italian. Tony is like that.

"What took you so long, did you get lost?" Marion asks.

"Well, just a little," I answer quietly with a weak smile. I'm embarrassed to admit that I got lost, as Tony's directions were quite simple. Our families have been close friends since 1968, so I feel very comfortable in their house. Tony diplomatically points out where the shower is in case I want to clean up. I guess the +100-degree heat had worked it's magic on my body, but it isn't bothering me. We go into the kitchen and he offers me a tall glass of chilled water. "Man, that tastes good," I tell him as we sit down at his kitchen table.

After a shower and some clean clothes, we hop in Tony's car and we drive over to his favorite casino to play poker. I played poker as a second job when I was a kid in the Navy. There's not much to do when you're out at sea for weeks at a time. We played the standard games

Saturday, September 6, 2003
Day Ten: Arrive Los Vegas, Nevada

usually with a $1 or $2 limit, but occasionally we played higher limits like $5 and $10. That's a lot of money when you're only making $90 a month. I haven't played much since those days.

I like to play standard, traditional poker games like draw, seven-card stud or low-ball and maybe one or two others, but not the crazy-ass games that so many guys play at home on Wednesday nights. These games have so many more wild cards and silly rules than standard games, only Einstein could figure the odds on drawing the right card.

Tony and I eat lunch while we wait for seats to open and then I play seven card stud, five-dollar limit with unlimited raises. Tony plays Texas Hold'em with a five-dollar limit. The neat part of playing at the casino is that no one needs to ante. So, you can afford to sit and wait for a decent hand without getting anted to death.

After four hours, I'm down $50 and Tony won $330, the lucky bastard. Actually, I know Tony is an excellent player. I did get three free Heinekens out of the deal, so I figure I only lost about 38 bucks, assuming four dollars per beer. Not a bad deal for four hours of relaxing fun. When we get back to Tony's place, Marion had washed my dirty laundry and prepared a tasty, homemade pasta dinner, topped off with her own delicious marinara sauce. The poker, the great dinner, some wine and good conversation made for a great day. Once in bed, I bring my journal up to date and decide tomorrow's destination will be Death Valley

Sunday, September 7, 2003
Day Eleven: Arrive Ridgecrest, California

After an oatmeal and banana breakfast, I check the bike over carefully, oil and tighten my chain, load on my luggage and head for Death Valley. When I gas up near the I-15 on-ramp, I ask a local guy for directions to Route 160 that leads to Death Valley. I know it isn't far away but I can't tell on my map. He confidently tells me, "Just head south on I-15, you'll see it. Route 160 isn't far." After miles of riding and no sign of Route 160, I know I've gone too far. How did I miss it? I stop near the California state line and ask directions from the counter clerk at an off-ramp gas station. This lady tells me I can keep going southwest another 60 miles on I-15 and when I get to a little town called "Baker," take Route 127 north. "It's a very scenic road and leads right into Death Valley," she cheerfully explains.

I follow her directions and as soon as I leave I-15 and head north on Route 127, I sense the heat and vacantness of the landscape. Dry, parched earth and sagebrush with mountains in the background is all I can see. After about 85 miles of very hot riding, I hit Route 190, which takes me to the Death Valley Visitors' Center. What a desolate landscape. Any plant life still attached to the ground looks dead. Rolling foothills of blue and grey dried, packed mud cover much of the view.

I see a vast desert with sand dunes, just like we've all seen in so many old movies. Now it is getting seriously hot; I don't know how hot, but I've never felt anything like it. I flip up my face-shield to get some fresh air and it feels like Kathy's hair dryer blasting right into my face. So, I quickly close it shut except for a small crack that I keep open with a clothespin. The ones I bought a few days ago at Dollar General, a smart buy except they eventually blow off and now I only have a couple left.

Fortunately, the bike's four-cylinder, water-cooled engine is still running at normal temperature, at least while I'm moving. I'm not concerned about it overheating in a traffic jam or busy intersection out here. At this moment, I feel like the only person on the planet. It's a relief to see a sign for the Death Valley Visitors' Center, so I pull in for a rest, some cold water and information. The first thing the receptionist does is sell me a Visitors' Pass. "Here, tie this to your handlebars," she

Sunday, September 7, 2003
Day Eleven: Arrive Ridgecrest, California

tells me, "Just in case you get stopped by a park ranger." That didn't seem very likely, but I gave her 10 dollars anyway. Motorcycle passes are cheap at half the price of cars.

Inside the Visitors' Center, I sip on a bottle of cold water and contemplate my next destination. I decide to continue west to the California coast and ride up Highway 1 from San Louis Obispo to San Francisco and visit the USS Hornet, my old aircraft carrier that is now a national museum. Following Route 190, I ride through Furnace Creek, Beatty Junction and Stovepipe Wells. I have no interest in stopping, I just want to get an overview of Death Valley. Still on Route 190, I head generally west into the Sierra Nevada mountain range. It's a 180-mile ride from the Visitors' Center to Ridgecrest, California, my next destination.

The road winds through 4,000-feet- high elevations with narrow two-lane roads and lots of sharp turns and switchbacks without guardrails. The turns frequently post speed limits of 15 mph and the edge of the road is like looking off a sharp cliff. I try my best to stay focused on the road and forget about the drop-offs. It's a lonely, stressful ride after hours of brutal heat in Death Valley. The traffic is light though. Apparently, this is not a popular highway, at least at this time of year. I've been following a lone pickup truck for quite a few miles now. The driver must be a local, familiar with this road because he drives fast and handles the sharp curves with complete confidence. It's all I can do to keep up with him...her. Eventually, I'm so fatigued, I decide to let him go. This driver is good and I'm tired.

Finally, I leave Route 190 and take Route 395 south to Ridgecrest, California. I'm totally beat now and still have another hour of riding to Ridgecrest, the next town with motels and restaurants. As soon as I hit the lower altitude with open, flat land, the wind picks up and one gust after another slams the bike. I wonder as I fight the wind, why I'm doing this. Why am I out here? Is it because I needed a challenge? Am I bored with my life? Today was indeed a challenge, riding through all kinds of weather and road conditions. This is a sports bike and I'm leaning on my arms, wrists and hands all day. If I weren't such a dickhead, I'd be riding a more comfortable motorcycle.

Well, in any event, I'm glad I saw Death Valley and did the whole ride. I'm starting to miss Kathy and Eddy. I miss feeling her next to me in bed at night. But now I'm way the fuck out here in California and it's kind of like I have this job to do. I have to ride my motorcycle around the country until I've seen it all and done it all. This is my third motorcycle trip to the west...two to California and one up through Montana and into Canada. I'll have about 30,000 U.S. touring miles when I finish, not much more of the west to see after that.

Idly, I wonder if I should ride up the coast of California to Washington and then across the top of the US on US 2 to Main, then down the East Coast back to South Florida. I don't know if I have enough time for that, besides it might be too cold up north. I'll probably just cut back east from the California coast on I-80 and visit Utah. This wind just won't let up. How much of a gust would it take to blow a motorcycle right off the road? I've never heard of it happening. But I do know a Harley rider that got the shit scared out of him in North Dakota by wind gusts. Scared him so bad he stopped going out west to ride with his buddies.

I enter Ridgecrest at 6:30PM, check into a Travel Lodge Motel and take a relaxing shower. I need it too because I feel like I have about an inch-thick layer of salt on my body from sweating all day. After the shower, I find a Denny's, eat a veggie burger, call Kathy, update my journal and fall asleep. What a day!

Monday, September 8, 2003
Day Twelve: Arrive San Luis Obispo, California

The morning finds me very rested, but the toilet is calling my name. On my way to the bathroom, I'm searching through my tank-bag which is lying on the floor, and guess what? No pre-moistened ass-wipes! They were there yesterday morning, what happened? The only place I parked yesterday for any length of time was the Visitors' Center in Death Valley. Someone rifled through my tank-bag and stole all ten packages of my ass-wipes! Is this possible? Why would someone do that? And in Death Valley, no less. What would a pre-moistened, ass-wipe thief be doing in Death Valley? I decide to clean my ass the old-fashioned way, with a hooker's bath by squatting in the tub and washing my ass and crotch with soap and water.

Next up, my usual and very outstanding, oatmeal breakfast at Denny's, followed by a visit to K-mart for a new supply of pre-moistened ass-wipes, and then back on Route 178 west to Bakersfield, California. The weather is on the cool side, but nice. Lots of open space, green farm crops and farther down the road, miles and miles of open prairie with cactus trees. Route 178 is a hilly, two-lane road with an additional passing lane every few miles. It passes about 90 miles below Mount Whitney, the tallest mountain in the US at over 14,000 feet and about 50 miles below the heart of Sequoia Valley. Ranches, cattle, and even cowboys rounding up steers on horseback occupy the scenery.

About 30 miles before Bakersfield, I ride past Lake Isabella, a gorgeous body of rich blue water surrounded on three sides by the Sequoia National Forrest foothills. It is busy with campers and RVs, but not so many as to detract from the beauty of the lake—a stunning sight indeed. I arrive in Bakersfield at about 11:30AM and realize it's time for an oil change. After gassing up, I ask the station attendant if she can direct me to a motorcycle dealer. To my surprise, she gives me real, simple directions to a nearby Honda dealer. About 90 minutes later, I'm on the road again with fresh oil in my crankcase. After talking to the Honda guy about my trip, I take his advice and head west on Route 58 to San Louis Obispo. This is where the scenic coastal highway begins that will take me to San Francisco, a beautiful ride, especially on a motorcycle.

Monday, September 8, 2003
Day Twelve: Arrive San Luis Obispo, California

To my surprise, Route 58 proved to be quite a ride. It is another one of those narrow two-lane roads through open farmland and ranches. But, it also leads to another range of low mountains and very twisty, narrow, two-lane roads with lots of switchbacks. The tight, twisty road lasts for 70 miles and it's a fun ride. Still, my arms and neck ache a little from working the throttle, clutch and brake while whipping the bike around slow vehicles and tight turns. I'm ready to relax a little.

I've got to do something about this motorcycle seat, the $10 Indian blanket I bought a few days ago blew away when I stood up on my foot pegs at 90 mph to let some cool air blow through my crotch. So now, I'm sitting on my testicles again and it really annoys me, especially at the end of the day. I'm pretty sure, now that I think about it, that I didn't use this after-market seat on my last trip out west, I used the stock seat and I never had this problem. I'm definitely going to fix this tomorrow.

I pull into San Louis Obispo at about 4:30 and check into a Travel Lodge Motel at $53 per night, not bad for a charming coastal town like this. After a warm shower, I call Kathy. She tells me she's decided to refinish the kitchen walls and she has an expert wall finisher coming in tomorrow to do the work. I think the kitchen walls look great, but I'm not about to argue the point. She also tells me I left my casual walking shoes at Tony's house. I need these, they're my only escape from my heavy motorcycle boots. Although I hadn't needed them since I left Tony's place, I need them right now. After my depressing talk with Kathy, I head into town, which is not very big, about six blocks by six blocks, but very upscale and pretty. It reminds me of the Hamptons on Long Island.

I park the bike and walk around town for a while just to look the place over. Lots of boutique style shops, excellent restaurants and cool looking bars with great beer selections. Most of the people around town are young, likely because of the university nearby. This is a great time to replace my walking shoes, I think, with so many stores to choose from. So, I enter a big sporting goods store and walk out with a

Monday, September 8, 2003
Day Twelve: Arrive San Luis Obispo, California

nice pair of low-cut sneakers on my feet and a big bag containing my heavy all-weather motorcycle boots. A few minutes later, I spot a friendly looking bar and order a beer. After my second beer, it becomes clear I'm not going to strike up any conversations, so I leave to find something to eat. I did enjoy the two black and tans though, the first since leaving home.

Down the street, I walk into a lovely, clean place called Fresh Foods Cafeteria and pay $7.75 for all the fresh food I can eat in one visit. The vegetarian selection is plentiful, almost over-choice for my simple palet. As I eat, I notice the place is full of young college kids, some of them doing homework while absentmindedly shoving food in their mouths. One of the kids sitting at the table next to mine starts chatting with me in between bites because he notices that I have an anti-theft device attached to my sneaker. I didn't realize it was there until he mentioned it. I conceal my surprise and laugh, confessing I just stole the sneakers. He laughs too, but I can tell he's not entirely sure if I'm kidding.

After dinner, I head back to the sporting goods store, where I bought the shoes since it was on the way to my bike. I show the anti-theft device along with my purchase receipt to the guy that sold me the shoes and two other employees joined us. Now they're debating over how I managed to leave the store without the alarm going off. They finally conclude that the footwear is too low on my body for the alarm to detect. I may be on to something here, a glitch that will allow me to get free shoes for the rest of my life. The attractive young girl at the checkout counter says, "Well sir, you can either take off the shoe or put your foot on top of the counter next to this gizmo and I'll take it off."

I lift my leg up to put my foot on the countertop and immediately start falling backward. To save myself, I grab hold of a turn-style holding a display of sunglasses. A second later, I'm sprawled out on the floor along with about 50 pairs of sunglasses. I can't help laughing to cover my embarrassment. "This is the kind of stupid accident that only happens in the movies," I tell the young sales guy as he pulls me up by

Monday, September 8, 2003
Day Twelve: Arrive San Luis Obispo, California

the arm. Staying long enough to help put the sunglasses back where they belong, I then make a quick exit before I destroy something else; I never thought buying a pair of sneakers could be so exciting.

With a little luck, tomorrow I'll visit my former Navy home, the Aircraft Carrier, USS Hornet CVS12. I lived on this ship for three and a half years from 1960 through 1964. I didn't know it at the time, but this was a very decorated ship. It served in World War II, the Korean War, Vietnam War, and picked up the returning Apollo 11 Astronaut capsule from the first moon landing in 1969 and again, the Apollo 12 Astronaut capsule in 1970. I later learned that the hornet was attacked 59 times and yet never damaged by a bomb, torpedo or Kamikaze aircraft. In addition to that, it shot down 252 enemy aircraft in one month during World War II.

There's more, but the point is, the ship has a lot of history. In 1991, it was designated a national historic landmark, and in 1998, it became a public museum. It may seem strange, but when I served on this ship, I didn't know any of her history and didn't really care. All I cared about was having fun, drinking and playing poker. It'll be interesting to see if I can remember where I ate, slept and worked. I was an Interior Communications Electrician; an IC Man.

We took care of the ship's gyrocompass navigation system, the crew's audio-visual entertainment equipment, telephones and alarm systems. It was nice duty at the time because our division was one of the very few that had air-conditioned workspaces. Air conditioning wasn't all that common in the early '60s on Navy Ships. The normal mode of cooling was big round air-ducts that blew fresh air into our sleeping quarters and most other living and working
spaces. They would inject a little fresh water into the blowers and that would make the air "feel" cooler. I wouldn't like it now, but in 1960, we didn't know any better and no one bitched about it.

Tuesday, September 9, 2003
Day Thirteen: Arrive Santa Cruz, California

Two doors from my motel, I find a great little café for breakfast. When I get back, the desk clerk gives me a bath towel after I offered to buy one. I'm determined to make my motorcycle seat more comfortable. So, in an attempt to duplicate the comfort of the 10-dollar Indian blanket that blew away, I fold and unfold the towel until I get it just right. Then, after positioning it on the seat and sitting on it a dozen different ways, I tape it in place with duct tape. "Now, this oughta keep the little fucker from blowing away," I say under my breath.

Next, I oil and adjust my chain and while I'm doing this, I'm thinking, it's probably about time for a new one. It needs to be adjusted because it stretches under the strain of acceleration. The harder the bike accelerates, the more stress on the chain. Eventually, the chain stretches too much and there's no more room to adjust it because I can only move the rear wheel back so far to take up the slack. Plus, after a while, the chain just loses its flexibility and at that point, it can freeze up, or god forbid, it can break. I never had one break.

I replaced this chain in Albuquerque on my '97 trip. I started hearing strange noises and took it to a bike shop, that's how I found out it was bad. It's a good idea to listen carefully to your motorcycle, like your body, it tells you things so you can fix the problem early enough to prevent a tragedy, much like our body gives us warning signs before a breakdown. Kathy never listens to our car no matter how much I talk about this. She just drives it until it doesn't run anymore, that's how she notices something is wrong.

With the mechanical stuff done, I load on my luggage and head north on the Pacific Coast Highway, also known as Highway 1. Kathy and I flew out here with our good friends, Tony and his wife, Marion in the early '80s. We rented a car and did this same ride to San Francisco, but it seems all new to me now. Highway 1 meanders along the ocean, threaded between rolling foothills, farmland and cattle. For the first several miles, there are lots of cattle grazing along the hillside pasture and strangely to me, they graze right along the ocean surf in a few spots. It's an unusual scene.

September 9, 2003
Day Thirteen: Arrive Santa Cruz, California

The weather's beautiful and I see a sign for "Morro Bay" and decide to take a look. Wow! This is stunning. Nestled between the highway and the ocean is this gorgeous blue-water bay. It's protected from the ocean by a barrier of small rolling hills that form an inlet at the north end. Lots of sailboats and
yachts are docked in the bay. Canoeing, camping and RV-ing are also very popular here. Highway 1 attracts a lot of sightseers, especially on a pretty day like this. It's also very popular with motorcyclists. The road is fun to ride and at times, challenging because of the tight curves and high, rugged cliffs. With several days of mountain riding under my belt, I can feel my confidence coming back. I was never an ace mountain rider, probably just adequate.

There aren't any twisty mountain roads in South Florida so, to hone my skills, a small group of us rode several times to the Carolina mountains and practiced. In the Carolina mountains, I scared myself silly a few times trying to keep up with the more seasoned riders. After that, I decided to get a little expert instruction and signed up for two motorcycle racing schools. They came to South Florida once every year and trained motorcyclists in the art of riding fast and safe. Now I know "fast" and "safe" on a motorcycle sound like mutually exclusive terms but not to the students that go to these classes.

I also went to Sebring International Speedway two times for what they called "Open Track Day" for motorcycles only. We had the whole track to ourselves with no limits on speed. That was fun. I probably learned more on the race tracks than in the mountains, because on the race tracks, everyone goes in the same direction. We wore a full-body racing suit and there were no stalled cars or wandering animals to worry about. With that kind of safety margin, it was a lot easier to go test my limits on fast turns.

In one school at Moroso Speedway, now West Palm Beach International Raceway, I still managed to crash, in spite of all the common-sense rules. It was toward the end of the day and I was getting cocky after a whole day of fun on my new '96 Suzuki, GSXR 750. It was

Tuesday, September 9, 2003
Day Thirteen: Arrive Santa Cruz, California

the street version of the current hottest bike on the professional race circuit. The rev limiter kicked in at 13,500 RPM. The bulk of power suddenly arrived in at 8,000 RPM and when that happened, the front end would frequently surprise me by lifting off the ground. I had lots of wheelies on that bike, not all of them intentional either. It was a real screamer.

Anyway, I was coming down a long straightaway that goes under the spectator bridge at about 100 mph. One guy was ahead of me before we headed into a left-hand turn. I knew this was a pretty good rider because I had been watching him all day and I wanted to beat him into the turn. I pegged the throttle and passed him just in time to hit my brakes for the left-hander. Well, passing this guy at warp speed, then breaking like a maniac for a sharp turn scared the hell out of me. I was suddenly over my head. About halfway through the turn, I did what every inexperienced rider does when he gets scared in a curve. I released the gas and touched the front brake lever with my fingers.

This, of course, was precisely the wrong thing to do. In an instant, the dynamics of the bike completely changed and I was ejected from my seat and sent bouncing across the asphalt. My pretty new GSXR 750 flipped over and slid like a hockey puck across a grassy field into a shallow saw-grass pond about a hundred feet away. I re-broke my collarbone and my racing outfit looked like they had been in a fight with a stump grinder, but other than that, the medics said I looked okay. At the end of the class, I found out that the track officials and the instructor had bets on another rider and me. The bet was, "Which one of these two idiots will be the first to crash?" I won. It cost me $1,200 to fix my bike.

One good thing did come out of that accident: I was on my Honda Blackbird 1100XX, the same bike I'm riding now, heading out to meet my riding buddies one Saturday morning. I spotted two Harley riders just ahead of me. 'If I'm fast enough,' I thought. 'I can pass them before I enter the I-75 on-ramp.' I dropped down into second gear at about 45 mph and gassed it. I was by them and onto the I-75 on-ramp

Tuesday, September 9, 2003
Day Thirteen: Arrive Santa Cruz, California

before I knew what happened. Just then, I realized, 'Oh shit, I'm into this turn way too fast.' I knew this because I was pushing the bike lower and lower to tighten up my turn and the bike still kept heading for the edge of the road, a bad sign.

At this point, the bike was leaning over so far, the lower body fairing, the bike's fiberglass side covering, was scraping the asphalt with just enough pressure to cause the front wheel to lose some traction. I could feel the front tire slide and grip, and slide then grip again. At the apex of the turn, I was maybe a foot from going off the pavement. My mistake at the Moroso racing school flashed across my mind. Consciously, and counter to all my survival instincts, I didn't ease off the gas or touch the brake. Instead, I applied some throttle, steady and gently, as I emerged from the turn and smiled with tremendous relief as the bike straightened up while wondering if I should check my underwear.

When I met up with my riding buddies that morning, I told them about my near-death experience and proudly showed them my damaged lower body fairing. They were amazed I wasn't in the emergency room. My earlier error at the track saved my ass, proving I can learn from my mistakes. Of course, not showing off in the first place would have been the more mature course of action.

Farther up the Highway 1, the scenery gets more spectacular. It's a rough and raw beauty with ragged cliffs meeting head to head with wild, pounding surf far below. Bikers are out in force enjoying the coastline ride and its hilly, twisty roads. Right now, I have to stop and pee. I see a bridge that crosses over a deep crevice along Highway 1. As I step down to get under the bridge and out of sight, my foot slips on the steep, loose, rocky surface. Without thinking, I grab at the nearest thing, a rusty iron rod sticking out of the earth, wrapped with barbed wire. I looked down. Shit! The slope goes straight down for about 200 feet, ending on the rocky surf. If I hadn't grabbed that steel rod, my motorcycle trip would have ended right here. That queasy, sick feeling swirled through my belly for a moment as I contemplated what could

Tuesday, September 9, 2003
Day Thirteen: Arrive Santa Cruz, California

have happened. How easy it is to die. I cut the palm of my hand on the barbed wire, but that seems like a small price to pay for saving my ass. In my first-aid kit, I locate a Band-Aid and then find a safer place to pee..

Continuing north on Highway 1 at four o'clock, it's getting cold. A light drizzle accompanied by an afternoon fog moves in. That's enough encouragement for me to knock off a little early and find a motel at the next exit a few miles up the road. I'm now about 90 minutes from San Francisco. I figure I can reach San Francisco in the morning, pay a visit to the USS Hornet and then, with a little luck, I'll be able to leave the Bay Area before the evening rush-hour and head west to Utah, on I-80, my next destination.

In the coastal town of Santa Cruz, I check into a clean looking motel along Highway 17. After I throw my saddlebags in the room and wash up, I walk down the street to a little neighborhood restaurant and order the closest thing I can find to a vegan meal, a mushroom burger. I order the burger without meat and eat a meatless, mushroom burger, a baked potato and a garden salad. Not too bad, it's warm and it's filling.

Around 5 o'clock, with a full belly, I head across the street from my motel to a little bar called "The Watering Hole." It's got a slap-board exterior with a helmsman wheel over the front door. It looks like it's been here for a while. I like the nautical look. Since this bar is right across the street from my motel, I can even see my bike through its open front door. Knowing I don't have to ride my bike back to my motel, I feel I can relax and enjoy myself.

Most nights on the road, I have a beer or two and meet someone interesting, someone with a story. I always look forward to this part of the day. The place has a shotgun interior with one long bar that makes a 90-degree turn into the far side of the room as you walk in.

I sit on the corner of the bar, near the front door, and I can look down its length. Late-day sunlight is still streaming in the open doorway along with some faint street noise. The weather is perfect. The bartender brings me my Heineken. I take a sip as I watch straight ahead at the two

Tuesday, September 9, 2003
Day Thirteen: Arrive Santa Cruz, California

women farther down the long side of the bar, both look to be in their thirties. One is chubby. Well, okay, she's fat; not distractingly blubbery fat, but more like extremely plump. The other one is quite thin and mildly attractive. The thin one is complaining that she was just dumped by her boyfriend and is crying on her friend's shoulder while being reassured that this is not the end of the world. The thin woman cries, "I'm ugly, look at me, who would ever want me, I'm a loser. I know that's why he left me, it's because I'm ugly."

"You know that's not true, why do you keep saying that shit?" Her friend replies, trying to cheer her up. The two guys sitting nearer to me, also on the long side of the bar, are listening to this conversation. I interrupt the girls long enough to tell the thin one that I thought she's wrong about her looks.

"You look pretty enough to me," I say, trying to make her feel better and lying just a little.

"Look at my face. Look at all these old acne scars, how can you say that?" she shoots back. I smile and keep my mouth shut. She's way down the bar, the lighting is dim and maybe she's right. I think I'll just drop it. I see something out of the corner of my eye. I turn to my left and look out the open front door and see this guy standing just outside the bar on the sidewalk. He wears a spooky hood that obscures his head and face, like the grim ripper. He's pulling a large overloaded handcart with his personal belongings and he's staring into the bar like he's looking for someone—or hoping for a handout. So, out of idle curiosity, I ask the bartender, "Do you know this guy?"

No, not really," she says. I watch the guy a little longer and he just stands there. At this point, I'm curious, so I walk outside to say hello. He turns to look at me. Now I can see his face under the hood. He's an intelligent looking black man, probably in his mid-forties. I ask him, "Do you need anything?"

"Yes, I could use fifty-cents," he says.

Even though he only spoke a few words, his diction is perfect, and his overall demeanor conveys a certain dignity. I'm thinking, this is

Tuesday, September 9, 2003
Day Thirteen: Arrive Santa Cruz, California

not your typical homeless person. I reach into my pocket for some change or a dollar bill; all I have are a wad of 20 dollar bills. I hand him a 20. Here, take this; maybe it will help you." It was spontaneous on my part. I don't usually go around handing out 20 dollar bills to strangers, but this guy seemed different. He stares at the twenty for a long moment and then shoves it in his pocket with a look of indifference. He gives me the impression he really doesn't care about the twenty; he only needed fifty-cents. Then he looks at me for a long moment, turns and walks away towing his cart. He didn't say thanks, fuck you, or goodbye, a very peculiar guy.

Back in the bar, I ask the bartender again if she knows anything about him. "Well," she looks up, drying a beer mug, "He's been coming around since before I started here. He's kind of an urban legend in that he was supposed to be a college professor and his wife and kids all died in some kind of freak accident. Then, he just snapped."

"Well, he seems intelligent and well spoken, maybe it's true," I speculate. Gazing around the bar again, my eyes come back to the two guys sitting just around the elbow in the bar, within arm's reach. They are just nursing their drinks and staring at the mirrored wall stacked with liquor bottles; they seem to have been here for a while and look to be in their early forties. I say "Hi," and ask them if they live here in Santa Cruz. Jack, a friendly sort, introduces himself and his friend, Bob. Then Jack tells me he and Bob grew up around here.

"We've been drinking here all afternoon," Bob tells me, abruptly. "But, we're getting hungry. I think we're gonna go find some food." Clearly, Bob is a little sloshed and Jack isn't far behind. They're still coherent, but some food wouldn't hurt them at this point. "Where are you from?" Bob asks.

"Fort Lauderdale, Florida," I answer. "I'm on a motorcycle vacation, just touring the country by myself." They both tell me this is the one thing they would love to do someday. Then Bob continues, telling me about the 1100 CC Honda cruiser he had in the early eighties and how much he loved that motorcycle. It caught on fire," he tells me

Tuesday, September 9, 2003
Day Thirteen: Arrive Santa Cruz, California

with sadness in his voice. "The damn thing just burned up. Man, I loved that bike." Then with a big grin, he continues, "I rode it all over the place. I wanna get a new one though and tour around the country…like you're doing." Bob tells me the long version of the Honda bike fire…twice. The story seems endless. I feel like…please, please, just shoot me before you repeat that one more time. Finally, I change the subject.

"What do you guys do for a living?" I ask.

"We're retired from the construction business." Jack answers and Bob smiles in agreement. I have to think they just want to impress me because I had told them I was retired and the word retired sounds better than unemployed or between jobs. I guess they are between jobs and have some savings. I don't press them on the subject. I answer their questions about the bike I'm riding: brand name, engine size, horsepower, etc. Bob is impressed and asks, "Where's your bike, man? I wanna see it."

It's right over there," I say, pointing to the motel parking lot through the open door, "That's where I'm staying."

Bob stands up and looks out the open front door, sees my bike and decides he's not interested in walking that far, likely because of his unstable condition. Jack and Bob then get into a lengthy discussion about their newly created dream of buying motorcycles and touring the country together.

"Hey Ken, give me your e-mail address," Jack says, "so, I can let you know when we're ready to leave." He says this like I'm going to just jump on my bike and take off as soon as I get his e-mail. But, I give him my e-mail anyway and just chalk it up to barstool fantasies. These are nice guys, like a couple of asshole buddies that are always ready for a good time. I had friends like this in the Navy…lots of crazy adventures and too much booze.

They finally leave to find some food, and in Bob's case, not a moment too soon. Now I'm back to listening to the two girls again. The slim girl is getting a good buzz going and her sense of humor is

Tuesday, September 9, 2003
Day Thirteen: Arrive Santa Cruz, California

emerging in spite of the sour attitude she has about her looks. The fat girl, more introspective, is a good conversationalist, but their conversation still centers around the thin girl's problems with men. Out of boredom, I ask a few questions and learn they're both employed by the same Catholic school. The plump girl is a sixth-grade teacher with four kids and her friend is single and works as a secretary in the principal's office.

The songs I played on the jukebox earlier ended and so I ask the girls if they want me to play anything special. "No, we like what you're playing," the fat girl tells me. So, I play some more Willie Nelson, Gordon Lightfoot and James Taylor. They had overheard some of my conversation with Bob and Jack so, the plump girl says, "How can you have fun riding all over the country by yourself, don't you get lonesome?"

"Well," I say thoughtfully, "Not really because when I travel by myself I always meet interesting people and I can do exactly as I please when I want to do it."

"Are you married?" She asks. "Yeah, 38 years," I answer. Now, I can guess what the next question will be. She doesn't disappoint. "Doesn't your wife mind that you're gone off by yourself so long?"

"A lot of people ask me about that," I tell her. "But no, she's okay with it. She rode with me on the motorcycle for several years and never got hurt. We had a lot of fun, but now she doesn't want to push her luck. Also, after thirty-eight years we pretty much understand and trust each other—so she lets me do my motorcycle thing. It's a good marriage."

She tells me she feels it would be a bummer traveling alone. "It's just too lonely," she repeats. I sit in silence for a few minutes listening to James Taylor sing "Walking Man."

This conversation causes me to think back. I met Kathy on a blind date arranged by mutual friends of ours. Meeting Kathy seemed so natural that I never gave it much thought about whether she was the right

Tuesday, September 9, 2003
Day Thirteen: Arrive Santa Cruz, California

girl for me to marry. I had never dated much in high school. In fact, I was a total flop with girls, to be honest.

A few months after we had been dating, I took off on a spur-of-the-moment road trip to California with my friend Doug, the guy that arranged our blind date. In Southern California, we partied with my old Navy buddies for a few weeks and then left for Greenwich, Connecticut where we got jobs and roomed on top of the bar Doug's older brother owned on Main street. Kathy and I were writing love letters back and forth and after I had been gone for about two months, I realized I really was in love and so did Kathy. When that longing for Kathy hit me, I left Doug and headed home. Later that year, December 26th, we got married. Nothing in my life before or after ever seemed so natural and right.

We both came from very poor families with fathers that had serious alcohol problems. This common background gave us both the incentive to make a better life for ourselves, which we did. I made a career in the life insurance industry and took a bunch of college courses related to my new career. Kathy went to the local college for an AA degree while raising our only child, a sweetheart little girl. In effect, we generally helped raise each other into well-rounded, responsible adults. Well, at least Kathy is a well rounded responsible adult. I am occasionally.

I walk into the unisex toilet to urinate and when I come back, a guy, about fifty with a trim physique is sitting on the stool next to mine. He orders a beer as I take my seat and we make eye contact. He says, "Hi." A few moments later, he asks where I'm from. I fill him in briefly on my trip and ask him if he lives around here.

"No, I'm just working in the area," he says. "I'm actually from Northern Washington State, not far from Seattle." After a little more give and take I find out the guy is living in the woods a few miles east of here in a 14-foot travel trailer with his best friend, a Border Collie. He tells me the company he works for was hired by the US Parks Service to build footpaths in the forest.

Tuesday, September 9, 2003
Day Thirteen: Arrive Santa Cruz, California

"Jesus, I didn't know there was such a job," I say. "No wonder you look like you're in good shape."

"Well, it helps," he smiles. He tells me he worked in the restaurant business for thirty years and although the money was okay, in the end, he hated it. "This is the first job I've ever had that I really love. I don't make any money," he smiles, "but I love this work." He chuckles and tips his beer in my direction. The guy is a real outdoors, nature-nut and he loves animals. We sip our beers and swap dog stories for at least a half hour. Finally, I look up and tell him, "You know, I just realized something—if it weren't for my greyhound, Eddy, keeping my wife company at home, she might have been reluctant to let me go on this trip. I owe one to Eddy!" I say with a hearty laugh.

"Here's to our dogs," he replies with a warm smile as we tip beers together for a toast. The footpath fellow swallows his last bit of beer and pays his bill. We say goodbye and I walk across the room to put two more dollars in the jukebox. As I walk back to my stool, my attention returns to the two women again. Since they work at a Catholic school, I ask them about their religion. It turns out that neither one of them are Catholic. But, this leads to another story about the heavy girl's five-year-old daughter.

She tells me, "One day, my daughter's uncle, her father's brother, came to our house for a visit. My little girl had never seen this man before. Well, as soon as she sees her uncle, and before she was even introduced, she tugs on my sleeve to get my attention and whispers in my ear, "Mommy, that man used to be my father." Then, privately, my daughter went on to tell me details about her memories of a previous life she had with this man that is now her uncle. And that's not all, because later, she made some more revelations about other family members she knew in her former life. We don't really know what to make of it, but we do think she has some special abilities."

"I don't know about special abilities," I tell her, "but childhood memories of a previous life are not uncommon. They usually appear between ages two and five. If I were you, I would ask her more

Tuesday, September 9, 2003
Day Thirteen: Arrive Santa Cruz, California

about what she remembers and write it all down because these past-life memories usually fade away by age seven. Also, people usually reincarnate in what are called soul groups, which would explain your daughter's prior lives with present family members. You should read up on the subject of reincarnation."

While we're talking about reincarnation, the slim girl is busy drinking and she has become more animated. She is smiling and swaying rhythmically to the music. It is like she totally forgot about her "ugly" issues and that her boyfriend dumped her. A minute later, the reincarnation conversation ends and I'm back to sipping my beer, listening to "Scotch and Soda" by the Kingston Trio.

A big, brawny guy with huge, beefy, tattooed arms, a shaved head and a plain white T-shirt that fits like a second layer of skin walks in and sits down right where Bob and Jack sat earlier. Scotch and Soda ends, so I drop another two dollars in the jukebox and punch in seven more songs. When I walk back to my stool, the big guy and I make eye contact, sort of acknowledging each other's existence with a small nod. He looks a little scary, the kind of person you don't fuck with.

Oddball people fascinate me, though, I can't help it. So, after a few minutes of staring at nothing, my curiosity gets the best of me. I make eye contact again and tip my beer…a silent hello. After a pregnant pause, we start talking a bit. He tells me he lives in the area and likes to come in here for a few drinks. A tattoo on his right bicep says, "ARMY" and another one, too faded to see clearly, looks like Vietnam. Others look like biker tattoos—the Harley rider kind.

"You were in Vietnam?" I ask. "

"Yeah, I was in 'Nam," he answers in a deadpan monotone. "I lost most of my eyesight in that war. So, I'm now classified as disabled."

"It looks like you were in the Army."

"Yeah, I was in the infantry…and I was there too long. We did a lot of bad shit in that country. A lot of bad shit I don't want to remember and don't want to talk about."

Tuesday, September 9, 2003
Day Thirteen: Arrive Santa Cruz, California

It sounds like he isn't in the mood to talk much, at least not about that subject. So, I shut up. This wasn't the kind of guy to push into a conversation. But after a few minutes, we make some small talk about motorcycles, riding the coastal highway, etc., and he starts to open up. I wonder how he could ride a motorcycle if he is almost blind—but later, I find out he still has one decent eye. The guy is tough, no doubt about it.

But he also has a lot of personal issues. Later, he confesses that he has a problem with alcohol and tells me he's been jailed a few times on drug charges. I notice he smokes like a New Jersey oil refinery and wonder about his life expectancy. "I still live the war every day," he tells me, "even in my dreams… it just never goes away."

Later, I learn more about his war injuries from bullet wounds and the shrapnel, which caused his eye injuries and injuries to his legs. He doesn't go into detail; he just spills a little here and there as we talk about music, politics and the Iraq war. He tells me, "Bush is an asshole. We had no business invading Iraq." That doesn't exactly surprise me based on his experience in Vietnam. Most Vietnam Vets I've met or heard in the media are against this war. We are in general agreement on most issues. We talk off and on for almost two hours while I keep the songs going on the jukebox, mostly Willie Nelson, Jimmy Buffet, James Taylor, and Kingston Trio. During a quiet moment, he looks at me and says, "I don't mind talking to you, you're a good listener."

"Thanks, you're an interesting person," I tell him. This guy makes me think, Vietnam really was a dirty rotten war. A lot of guys got body-fucked and mind-fucked over there and never got over it. I've read about these hard luck cases, seen them in movies and TV documentaries, but that's it…I don't meet many in person, at least not like this guy. So many lives down the toilet. Fortunately for me, I got out of the Navy in November '63, just as the war was kicking into gear. I missed the whole thing

I see it's eleven o'clock and I should be thinking about getting some shuteye for my morning ride into San Francisco. But first, I have to pee. While I'm staring into the urinal, trying to direct my stream into

Tuesday, September 9, 2003
Day Thirteen: Arrive Santa Cruz, California

the little drainage slits at the bottom of the bowl, I hear this outburst back at the bar. "Fuck you! I'm not drunk and I'll leave when I'm fucking well ready to leave." I zip up my fly, open the door

Now totally shitfaced, the thin girl quite literally fell off her bar stool and is sprawled out on the floor. Her girlfriend is trying to pick her off the floor by the arm, telling her it's time to leave.

"Leave me alone goddammit, I'm fine," she shouts while vainly attempting to re-establish her dignity and stand up by herself. With a little assistance and more cajoling from her friend, she reluctantly stumbles toward the door.

When the door shuts, there is a moment of dead silence, like the quiet after a quick but furious thunderstorm. Even the jukebox is quiet. I had been playing it all night, kind of like an informal DJ. The Vietnam vet takes out his wallet. I'm sure it's because he wants to give me two bucks to play seven more songs on the jukebox and break the stillness. Quietly, he opens his billfold and looks inside, pauses, and then closes it, putting it back in his jeans. I was close enough to see he only had three ones left. He can't even afford another beer. So, I play another round of tunes and tell the barmaid "I'd like to buy my friend here a beer."

After a few more minutes of small talk, I take the last swallow of my Heineken, bid farewell to the Army guy and walk across the street to my motel room. As I lie in bed writing in my journal, I think how lucky I am to meet these fascinating characters on my journey.

Wednesday, September 10, 2003
Day Fourteen: Arrive Fairfield, California

In spite of all the beers last night, I feel entirely normal this morning. In fact, I feel great. All I want right now is something to eat. I'm going to get breakfast. The desk lady at the motel suggests I try the café around the corner. "Just take a left at the traffic light," she says. It turns out to be an old warehouse district that has been converted into shops and eateries. I find the café; it's cafeteria style with a big outdoor patio. I order granola cereal with soy milk. Soy milk! A restaurant with soy milk. Wow! I get some thick and crunchy whole wheat toast with fruity jam along with a generous serving of tasty little red potatoes sliced and cooked in a light, olive oil and seasoned just right. Plus, I have a cup of very fresh fruit. What a great breakfast!

When I get back to the motel, I tell the lady at the front desk, "I want to kiss you for sending me to that café with the great food."

"No," she says, very formally. "A simple thank you will do just fine."

I think I scared her a bit. California always seems light years ahead of other states on most everything except, maybe, managing their budget. So, who's perfect, right? Now I just have to pack my luggage and head for Alameda, Naval Air Station in San Francisco to find the USS Hornet. By nine o'clock, I'm back on the scenic coastal highway. It's downright cold. I stop and put on my liner, my scarf and my raincoat to keep out the cold air. Now I'm warm. The ride is thoroughly enjoyable.

Oh shit! As I head down a steep hill, I see it at the bottom, just waiting to spoil my perfect morning—a horrible thick, gray fog. I'm now steering the bike and wiping the moisture off my face shield. After a while, my glasses fog up too, so I have to pull over before I go blind all together. I hate fog! I go through this stop-and-wipe procedure one more time and then bingo, I'm out of the fog and on a high altitude, narrow, twisty piece of highway. The air is still heavy with morning dew and the road is slick. On a tight curve, the bike is leaned over a bit. Suddenly, my tires slide over the slippery painted centerline in the middle of the road. It feels like the bike is sliding out from under me. But, the tires quickly regain their grip and the slide stops. I yank the bike

Wednesday, September 10, 2003
Day Fourteen: Arrive Fairfield, California

back to my side of the road. My stomach feels a little unsettled again. Death sometimes seems so near.

Entering San Francisco, I immediately lose my bearings because I'm overwhelmed by the morning traffic. Suddenly, I have no idea where I'm going because I can't read the road signs and steer through traffic at the same time. And, it's not a good idea to look at maps in dense traffic while piloting a motorcycle. Finally, I find a place to pull over and check my map. I get back on the bike and within a mile, I'm lost again. San Francisco highway signs look like Greek when I'm moving along with dense, high-speed traffic.

Once I get off the freeways, it's less intense and I can stop and ask directions from pedestrians. Finally, I find it, the USS Hornet CVS 12. It looks just like I left it 40 years ago and in the same location too, Alameda Naval Airbase. It's a big ship, 893 feet long, and believe it or not the top speed on this old girl was 34 knots. That's 39 mph, pretty damn fast for an old ship that weights 40,000 tons.

At certain scheduled times, the captain would do what's called a "Full Power Trial." That's Navy jargon for a top-speed run. The damn thing shook so much, trash cans would move across the floor, pencils and pens rolled off the desks. It generally felt like the ship was coming apart at the seams, mainly because back in those years, the technology for balancing four 27,000 pound propellers was in its infancy. It was exciting though. It's hard to forget the tremendous power of four 37,500 horsepower steam turbines at full power on the open sea. In case you want me to add it up for you, that's 150,000 horsepower.

Once onboard, I see the same ugly, green tile with white specks covering the passageway floors, "decks" in Navy talk. I find my old sleeping quarters; the same Spartan bunks stacked four high. The only change I notice is in the heads (bathrooms) and it is superficial; they put privacy curtains in front of the toilet stalls. Actually, they were plastic shower curtains. When I used those toilets, there were no privacy curtains. It wasn't unusual to stare into the face of another guy, an arm's reach in front of me, as he sat on his crapper. And

Wednesday, September 10, 2003
Day Fourteen: Arrive Fairfield, California

yes, we could watch each other wipe our asses, we usually diverted our eyes, however. Most guys carried little paperback novels in their back pockets so they would have something else to look at while they used these toilets. It was a good idea to know when the bathrooms weren't too busy. Right after breakfast, lunch or dinner was unfortunate timing, and smelly also.

After a few dead-ends, I find the crew's mess hall, where we ate three meals a day on eight by three-foot foldup tables. This is also where I took my GED test after quitting school to join the Navy. I was 17 and only had peach fuzz to shave in the morning.

The lower decks, where I worked most of the day, are dark and not restored for visitors so I can't go down there. I can, however, go on a guided tour of the engine rooms with the other tourists. There are two engine rooms, each with two of those 37,500 horsepower steam turbine engines I just mentioned. The guide I join up with takes my tour group to one of these engine rooms and explains how it all works. I'm the only one in the group, including the tour guide, that had actually served on the ship. I was still very familiar with these engine rooms because I used to come down here to visit my buddies and work on their communication systems.

As the tour guide goes through his presentation, I keep my mouth shut and listen...for a while. But, the temptation to add a little color to the tour guides talk finally overtakes me, and I raise my hand to say a few words. I tell the group I served on the ship and went on to describe how loud and hot it was in these spaces.

"How loud was it?" I ask rhetorically. "Well, it was so loud that we had to yell at the guy standing right next to us, and hand signals were a common practice. And how hot was it? Well, 110 degrees was not uncommon. If that wasn't exciting enough, now and then a steam fitting would malfunction, causing a deadly burst of steam that would sometimes cut through some poor sailor's arm, leg or torso."

From the tour guide's look, I don't think he wants me to go on any longer, so I shut up. But it's hard because all the memories are

Wednesday, September 10, 2003
Day Fourteen: Arrive Fairfield, California

flooding back. I remember these engine rooms being cooled with the same ventilation system as our sleeping quarters. They used big overhead air-ducts with water-injection systems to make it feel cooler than the actual temperature. The engine rooms also contained salt-tablet dispensers to replenish the salt lost from heavy perspiration. The sailors would take about one tablet per hour while on their shift.

The best memories of my three years on this ship were out at sea. On Sundays, I recall taking my favorite book and bunk blanket out on the catwalks that run along the side of the flight deck, getting real comfortable and reading. I read a lot of books on that ship, and sometimes I'd get lucky and see a pod of dolphins pacing alongside us, playing with each other. Sometimes, a pod of whales would raise their giant bodies above the water and check us out too. I guess they were curious about all the noise and activity caused by four giant underwater propellers that each weighed more than 27,000 pounds. Not to mention the noise from jets, helicopters and propeller planes that were regularly landing and taking off on training exercises.

At sea, I spent most nights playing poker, usually one-dollar limit and a quarter ante. On rare occasions, we played for higher stakes. That was my passion, playing poker. On our six-month cruise to the far east, I won $1,700, all of which I spent in Japan, Hong Kong and the Philippines. I bought Noritake China for my mother, a fancy camera for myself and a complete state-of-the-art stereo component system. The rest I wisely invested at the bars and on the very sweet Japanese bar girls.

Japan is where I lost my virginity at age nineteen. It was the most amazing experience of my life up to that point. When I told my shipmates, I couldn't shut up about how great it was. I guess it was fairly obvious to them I had been a virgin up to that day. Most of the girls that worked the bars would take the sailors back to their own apartment. There, we would take a bath together with lots of playful laughing and rubbing, followed by a massage and great sex…with no rushing. For a few extra bucks, we could take the whole night. It was an extraordinary experience for a nineteen-year-old kid like me. I didn't

Wednesday, September 10, 2003
Day Fourteen: Arrive Fairfield, California

learn anything about how to become a skilled lover, but that wasn't the girl's job. I would have to learn that on my own.

At that time, we only had to deal with venereal diseases a shot of penicillin would cure. Fortunately, that only happened to me once and it was a very mild case, just a simple infection. Some of the guys had two or three types of VD...at at the same time. They bragged about it like it was a noteworthy achievement. Sex while on board the ship was pretty much limited to our shower time. The standard Navy joke was, "It's my dick and I'll wash it as fast as I want too, thank you very much!"

On the way back to the states, my poker winnings took a dive. I had spent all my prior winnings and was a $1,000 in the hole when we got home, mostly with IOUs. However, between my meager paychecks of about $90 a month and better results in my card games, I paid it all back in about two months. I had become a little overconfident.

It's almost time to leave my old Hornet and get back on my bike. I take a few pictures for memories, buy a book of the ship's colorful history and walk onto the gangplank. Now it's time to get out of the San Francisco area before the late-day traffic rush. This turns out to be more difficult than it sounds because right off, traffic is dense and fast and I miss a couple of critical turns. Rush hour traffic starts early here.

Now, I'm stuck at the entrance of a big toll bridge. I don't want to go over, but I have no choice (It's not the San Francisco Bay Bridge, I did that one coming in). So, I pay the two-dollar toll and tell the toll guy I'm lost. He writes me a note so I can get my two dollars back and says, "Go over the bridge, turn around and come back. When you get back to this toll booth, take this note to the office right over there and they'll refund your two dollars." That works out okay and I head for I-80 West, but I'm confused and overwhelmed by the dense, fast traffic and unfamiliar roads and miss my turn onto the I-80 West on-ramp.

I manage to turn around without getting creamed by a speeding car and finally make it onto I-80 East only to get bogged down in rush hour traffic. I'm now crawling along at 40 mph and next to me, I notice the HOV lane; those cars are speeding by me at about 70 mph. A gray-

Wednesday, September 10, 2003
Day Fourteen: Arrive Fairfield, California

haired woman, about sixty, in an old Mercedes sedan, pulls up next to me on my right. She points and yells for me to go left. I look left and see the cars speeding by in the HOV lane. I flip up my face-shield and scream, "Okay to use the HOV lane?" She nods, 'Yes.'

An anxious glance back for oncoming HOV traffic indicates I should have enough space. I downshift and take off like I've been shot from a bazooka. In a flash, I'm doing eighty-five in the HOV lane. I slow down to about seventy as my adrenaline also settles. When I glance back, it makes me queasy to see how easily I could have misjudged and become the hood ornament on the big black Lincoln Navigator that is right on my ass. How did he get here so fast? About thirty minutes out of San Francisco heading east, the HOV lane on I-80 ends and I hit even worse rush hour traffic in Fairfield, California. My body is screaming, 'I'M HUNGRY!' And the late afternoon sun is oppressively hot. I decide to stop for the night, eat, do my laundry and head out for Utah in the morning. The Inn of America looks good. After checking in and unloading my gear, it's five o'clock.

Now for some food. In a strip shopping center close by, I find a Chinese restaurant, not my favorite cuisine, but sometimes it's okay. Not this place though, the food tastes like shit. I half expect the waiter to read my mind and say, "What do you expect sir, it is shit." The stuff on my plate looks vaguely like broccoli and white rice and it's loaded with some kind of sweet, gooey brown syrup. I'm hungry though, so I eat every bit of it and after that, I'm still hungry. So, I walk two doors down to a Subway shop and get a foot-long, veggie sub and devour it like a hungry wolf. Now I feel much better and can think of something else besides my stomach.

Back at the motel, while I'm doing my laundry, the guys-next-door are having a three-man party on the sidewalk outside their room. The biggest fellow, about 40, acts as the leader. He has long, dirty-blond hair. Tattoos cover his arms, chest and probably some other areas not available for observation. His mannerisms remind me of Jeff Bridges' character, "The Dude" in *The Big Lebowski*.

Wednesday, September 10, 2003
Day Fourteen: Arrive Fairfield, California

They have a portable CD player lying on the grass in front of their room playing Johnny Cash tunes, and each guy has a can of Bud. As I walk by with my laundry, they know I'm on the Blackbird parked in front of my door and "The Dude" offers me a can of Bud. This isn't the time to be a beer snob, so I say, "Yeah, okay. Let me throw these in the washer and I'll be right back. Thanks!"

I hang out and bullshit with them until my laundry is done. "The Dude" is from upstate New York and shows me a picture of his Harley Fat Boy all tricked out with custom paint and lots of chrome. I ask him why they are here and he says, "We remove tree roots from municipal sewer systems; we do it all over the country."

Now I've met two people with occupations that involve trees. These guys remove roots from subterranean sewer systems, and the man from the bar in Santa Cruz-cuts down trees to make foot-paths in the forest. You don't meet people like this very often. "The Dude" points to their trucks, a stone's throw away and says "I've been with the company for five years. I like it because they leave me alone and the money's good." Of the other two men, one looks like a smaller version of "The Dude" and about the same age, but with shorter hair. The third fellow is in his late twenties. He's clean-cut, more like an insurance salesman. He doesn't fit with the other two, but they don't seem to mind.

Thursday, September 11, 2003
Day Fifteen: Arrive Bishop, California

Today is the anniversary of 9/11. I get on the road at 9AM after another Denny's breakfast. The weather is beautiful. The bike is running well and sounds frisky in the fresh morning air. From Fairfield, I head east on I-80 to get on Route 50 which passes by the outskirts of Sacramento, then onto Route 88, then onto Route 89 and finally Route 395 South. By the time I hit Route 395, I need gas. At the gas station, I lay my eyeglasses on the back part of my seat, the part I don't sit on. Then I take off my helmet and start talking to two guys on Harleys.

One fellow, short-ish, maybe five-foot-seven, is from California and rides a big Harley. The other one is extremely tall, like six-foot-eight, I kid you not, and movie star handsome. He has a German accent and tells me he's from Germany. He is riding a small Harley 883 Sportster. He must have been a bit self-conscious about riding the little Harley because he made a point of telling me that he had a new Harley Soft-tail Custom back in Germany. That's a full-sized Harley. Anyway, when we say goodbye, these guys ride off and together, they look like a comedy act headed for Vegas with the big fellow riding a little Harley, his knees high up in the air and the small guy riding the big Harley.

After they take off, I finish gassing up and get back on my bike. When I take off, things just don't look right. I feel my face to see if my glasses are on. No, they're not! I pull over on the shoulder and slowly walk back to the gas station scanning the blacktop for my glasses along the way. I know I placed them on my seat when I filled up, I remember that much. The young fellow at the service station tries to help me find them, but no luck. Now I feel brilliant that I bought an extra pair of glasses just for this trip. So, I fish my spare eyes from my tank bag. Wow, what a difference! I can see! Now, maybe I can find the glasses I lost. Walking back to my bike, I scan the ground for my glasses, only this time, I can actually see things. They must have fallen off my seat onto the road when I left the station. Sure enough, I spot them in the center of the road...but it's too late. They look as flat as a razor blade. I put them in a plastic sandwich bag for memory's sake.

Thursday, September 11, 2003
Day Fifteen: Arrive Bishop, California

It's not much longer and I'm riding through the Sierra Nevada Mountains at altitudes of 7,000 to 8,000 feet. This section of Route 395 is full of twisty, curvy roads. The weather is gorgeous and considering it's a weekday, there are quite a few motorcycles on this route. You know you're on the best roads when you see so many other bikers.

At a highway construction site, I have to wait about 20 minutes for a lead-vehicle to take us to the other end of the road work. While I'm waiting, I strike up a conversation with the motorcyclist next to me. He's on a 1993 Suzuki 1100 sport-touring bike. He tells me he's from Massachusetts and is about halfway through a six-week tour of the US. He's doing it alone, like me. This is only the third long-distance biker I've met so far. These people are hard to come by. We share some traveling stories and he tells me more than anything, he hates riding in the rain. "I'll take the cold any day over the rain," he says.

"I hate fog," I tell him. "Because it makes me go blind." He tells me he's very familiar with my bike because his friend back in Mass has a Blackbird, just like mine. About that time, the lead-vehicle arrives and takes us past the construction area and we share a spectacular ride down the mountain together, parting company with a hand wave.

After the Suzuki rider splits off, I stay on Route 395 South. Now I'm directly east of San Francisco. Yosemite National Park is on my right and the Nevada State Line is a few miles to my left. As I descend from the upper elevation of the Sierra Nevada Mountains on a big four-lane road with a long sweeping turn, I'm looking for Lake Mono, I remember it from my last trip out west. There it is on

my left. It's absolutely beautiful! I have to be careful I don't run off the road staring at it because it's so strikingly big…and blue.

The snow melting off the High Sierra Mountains feed Lake Mono each Spring. The secluded, sky-blue body of water looks other-worldly nestled at the base of this mountain pass and surrounded by a broad band of pure-white shoreline. Within this body of blue are swatches of saw-grass and hundreds of unusual rock formations that

Thursday, September 11, 2003
Day Fifteen: Arrive Bishop, California

poke above the water, some of which spread onto the pearly white shoreline. Over the years, the lake has been a great source of dispute between developers that need the water and conservationists that want to protect its natural beauty. It's easy to see why California tree-huggers don't want this place fucked with.

    I pull into the Visitor's Center for a rest and a chance to get a better look. Then, back on the bike for my final 30-mile ride south to Bishop, California where I'll stay for the night. I know the place because the Honda shop here repaired my Blackbird back in '97 when I crashed it on Route 120, a little north of here. It was the owner of the Honda Shop that drove out to the crash site and hauled me and my wrecked bike back 50 miles to Bishop.

    On my way into town, I stop in and ask the young female counter clerk if I can say hello to the owner. "He won't be in until the morning," she tells me. He's at a Honda convention in Las Vegas. Oh well, maybe I'll stop by on my way out in the morning. I ride around back to ask the mechanic about the wear on my chain. He remembers me and my bike. I ask him if he thinks I need a new chain yet. He looks it over kind of quickly, wiggles it a little and says, "Nah, you got quite a few miles left on this one." That settles it in my mind, at least for the time being.

    Riding down the main street, I spot "The Outdoorsman Motel." The price is $53, a little pricey but the other places are about the same, so I check-in. After taking a shower, I call Kathy. After some sweet small talk, she tells me everything is okay…no problems. I'm always happy to hear that. Now, I think I'll walk down the street to get a beer. A busy Mexican restaurant catches my attention. Taking a seat at the long bar with about thirty stools, all occupied, I order a Heineken. "No Heineken," she announces. So, I order a Dos Equis.

    The two men next to me are friends in the middle of a long conversation about horses. I sip my beer and listen. When they run out of conversation, I say to the fellow next to me, "I couldn't help but overhear that you two are really into horses and ride a lot." Then I ask,

Thursday, September 11, 2003
Day Fifteen: Arrive Bishop, California

"Do you have any dogs?" He answers, "Oh yeah, dogs, horses, cats, llamas, wives, children, you name it."

"Well," I say, "I've always wanted to ask a real horse and dog person like you a question. What's smarter, a horse or a dog?"

"Well," he pauses to think. "They're both smart in their own way."

"Yeah," I persist. "But if you had to pick just one, the horse or the dog, which one would you say is smarter?"

"Okay, I guess the dog is smarter," he says. "But, horses are smart too, you just have to understand them...and most people don't know how to do that."

These guys go on to tell me they're both from San Diego. They're both independent business owners and they're here with their horses to do trail riding. We talk about horses, dogs, cats and llamas and the California recall election for about an hour. They both think businesses are leaving California because of the ridiculously high worker's compensation premiums that employers have to pay. Additionally, they both want to get rid of Governor Gray—not a popular governor.

After they leave, I order a veggie burrito, without cheese or sour cream from the bartender. Did you ever get the feeling that maybe you picked the wrong restaurant? Well, I have that feeling about this place. The bartender takes my order, but she seems overworked, in a dither. When I really start to pay attention, I notice, the whole place seems disorganized, busy and chaotic. Okay, I'm here, so what the hell, I'll follow the path of least resistance and eat here.

After about twenty minutes and no food, I start getting antsy. The waitress, who has been avoiding eye contact, starts to feel guilty and tells me, "Not much longer." Then, after 30 minutes, she's avoiding eye contact again. After almost 40 minutes, she finally delivers my burrito with an apologetic look. And, no real surprise, it's dripping with cheese. I should have listened to my inner voice. So, I remind the waitress about the "no cheese" request saying, "Look, I'm sorry, I just don't eat cheese."

Thursday, September 11, 2003
Day Fifteen: Arrive Bishop, California

She says, "Damn, I told the cook no cheese, you want me to take it back? Thinking things can only get worse from here, I say, "no, how about we just call it even, I'll pay for my beers and eat somewhere else." She actually seems relieved, so I leave her a generous tip and walk out. I feel sorry for the woman. Down the street, I see a restaurant I had considered earlier and passed up because it looked too quiet and there was no bar. Inside, it has a Southern California look and when I check out the menu, it has my kind of food. I order a veggie burger with a side of asparagus and a gourmet quality garden salad. The waitress is outstanding because she seems to know what I want before I order. And, she makes me feel like I'm her only customer. I'm not though, because the place is now bustling. When she brings the bill, I say, "Hey, anyone ever tell you that you're a damn good waitress?"

"Oh, thank you," she smiles appreciatively.

"No, really, I'm serious. I got the feeling you knew exactly what I wanted and you made me feel like I was your only customer, even though the place is packed."

"Wow! Thanks for the compliment," she smiles again.

"You should be in one of the helping professions, like medical care or nursing."

"Thank you so much. I needed a morale booster right now," she says and then goes on to tell me she's planning to start college soon and says, "It's strange you mentioned the healthcare industry and nursing because that's what I'm looking into right now." Back in my motel room, with a full belly, I update my journal for an hour and fall asleep.

Friday, September 12, 2003
Day Sixteen: Arrive Saint George, Utah

After a sound sleep and Denny's breakfast, I sit on the bike and my ass gets wet. Last Friday, I folded up a towel and taped it to my seat, so I wasn't sitting on my testicles. That worked out pretty well, except the morning dew soaked into the terry cloth towel. I tried covering the seat overnight, but I can't remember to do that all the time. Not only that, after a whole week, the duct-tape has stretched and the towel has shifted. Here is what I'm going to do, I am replacing it with a new towel and this time, I'm covering the entire towel with duct tape so the moisture and rain can't soak through. After this, all I have to do is wipe the moisture off the duct tape. Hell, this thing is evolving into a whole new seat.

    The wind still bothers my left shoulder blade though. So, rather than wear the small towel as a scarf, I'm laying it over my left shoulder under my jacket, so it covers my left shoulder blade. It feels like a hot knife when the wind blows down my back but only on my left side. I figure it's probably stage-four bone cancer in my left shoulder blade. I just have to have it confirmed by a doctor. I like to assume the absolute worst, then things can only improve from there.

    Again, I stop by the Honda Motorcycle shop to say hello to the owner, Randy, because I missed him last night, but he is still not in. The young counter girl says he's still in Las Vegas. I buy a can of chain oil, which I need anyway and ask the counter clerk to tell Randy I said hello. Back on the road with clear weather, my destination today is the Little Ali-Inn in Rachel, Nevada. I head west on Route 6 to Route 120, which takes me right past the place I crashed this bike in 1997. This brings back a slew of memories.

    On that trip out here in '97, I was depressed, in my mid-fifties and dealing with my existential midlife crisis. Motorcycles gave my life meaning, excitement. Speeding gave me the rush I needed to stay alive and I looked for any excuse to speed. One afternoon, I was heading west on Route 82, a two-lane road to Roswell, New Mexico. I passed a small batch of cars headed in the opposite direction. I was doing 110 mph and at the tail-end of those cars was a Texas State Trooper. Oh shit! I looked in my mirror and sure enough, I saw his brake lights go on. He was

Friday, September 12, 2003
Day Sixteen: Arrive Saint George, Utah

turning around to chase me. I didn't wait, I kicked my speed up to 135 mph and kept it there, racing west for the New Mexico State line about 50 miles away. I never saw the trooper again. He probably gave up before he really started, but it was fun for me.

In the rural ranch lands, off Route 82 in Roswell, New Mexico, a UFO crashed in July 1947. The story, released by the commanding officer of the local Army-Air Force base, ran in the newspapers. A few days later, the military officials in Washington changed the crash story from a flying saucer to a weather balloon.

Even before the story changed, air-tight government security was set up around the farm on which the crash occurred. Something was taken away in trucks. Locals witnessed the trucks. Area ranchers and former military people saw the wreckage and the bodies. Through the years, in spite of death threats, these witnesses have come forward and told their stories. A couple of these stories were deathbed confessions. Films and documentaries were made about the crash. Today, most experts that have truly researched the story agree that a weather balloon did not crash in Roswell.

After visiting Roswell's UFO museum, which is a light-hearted dedication to the 1947 UFO crash, I headed north on Route 285 for Santa Fe. A few miles out of Roswell, cruising again, at 110 mph I passed another small group of cars headed in the opposite direction. Once again, the last car in the group was a state trooper. Impossible! Not again! As soon as I whizzed by him, I saw his brake lights flash-on in my rearview mirror. He was turning around to chase me. Immediately, I sped up to 150 mph and held it there for several minutes enjoying the rush, until he was out of sight. Then I settled back to 135 for the next fifteen minutes or so. I figured unless the trooper called ahead for help, I would never see him again...and I never did. I made good time to Santa Fe that afternoon.

During hot summer days, dust devils are a common sight in the Nevada Desert. Most of them are small, just little swirling funnels of dust and wind alongside the road. However, a well-developed funnel can

Friday, September 12, 2003
Day Sixteen: Arrive Saint George, Utah

go as high as 100 feet or more and generate wind speeds of 60, up to 75 mph. I had never seen a huge one...until my 1997 trip. This was a different kind of dust devil. It was on the road, straight ahead of me. Dust devils were all over the place that day because it was so dry and hot on the Nevada desert but this one was huge, the biggest one I ever saw. The lower portion was shaped like a brownish-gray ball about one-and-a-half times the width of the road. Debris was flying all around it. The thing looked to be about a half-mile ahead and just hanging there in my path. Of course, the intelligent thing to do would be to stop and let it pass. Nah, that would be too logical...and boring.

I thought, Oh fuck it! I think I'll go through it and see what happens. Looking back, it's hard to believe I actually did this. I looked down at the speedometer, I was cruising at 110 mph. My heart started pounding. Should I maintain my speed, slow down or speed up? Faster is better, less chance of getting blown over, more stability. But how fast? Oh, 135 should do it. I kicked the speed up to 135, positioned the bike a few inches to the right of the centerline so I'd have about an equal chance of getting blown off either side of the road, then I tucked my head behind the low, sweptback windscreen...and in that little pocket of stillness, I listened to my heartbeat.

Wham! It felt like I passed through a time-warp and into a different dimension. When the dust cleared, I looked up and the bike had moved several feet to the wrong side of the white centerline, headed into oncoming traffic. Fortunately, there was no oncoming traffic. And strangely, nothing happened, even my luggage was still intact. The '97 trip was a lot of fun, but deep down inside, I knew I was asking for it.

Shortly after the dust devil incident, on a desolate stretch of two-lane road in the Painted Desert, I stopped to take a picture of the red, weather-etched plateau and pee. Just as I was getting back on my bike, a late-model Volvo Station Wagon zipped by in my direction. Back on the road, it wasn't long before I spotted the Volvo up ahead. I figured I would just zip by him like I did all the other cars and go on. This car was different though, the faster I went, the faster he went. He appeared to be

Friday, September 12, 2003
Day Sixteen: Arrive Saint George, Utah

accelerating to prevent me from passing him. Some people like to play that game...how fast do I have to go before the person behind me gives up? He picked the wrong idiot to play this game with.

I kept a respectable distance behind, but close enough, so he knew I was still in the game. After a few miles, we were going 110. I wondered how fast he'd be willing to push it. It appeared 110 was it. Now, it was my turn to show him what "fast" is. I dropped from sixth gear to fourth gear and nailed the throttle open. When I screamed past him, I was doing 150 mph and hit better than 160 before slowing to look back. I was so far ahead, I couldn't see him, so I slowed back to my usual cruising speed of 110.

I thought I would never see the Volvo again. However, a little later, when I was filling up my gas tank, a Volvo pulled up to the row of pumps on my right. Yeah, it was the same car. The man gassed up and while he was filling his tank, he looked at me. When his tank was full, he slowly walked over to my bike. I was busy washing my helmet's faceshield. At this point, I was a little nervous because maybe I scared him or his wife by screaming by him at 11,000 RPM and I could have pissed him off. The fellow looked at my bike and asked, "What kind of bike is this?"

"It's a Honda Blackbird 1100 CC, a new model," I answer.

Oh, I was just curious," he replies, eyeing my bike, "because I have a bike at home, a BMW and it's pretty fast. But, I have to tell you, I thought I was really hauling ass back there on the desert. But, when you passed me, you made me feel like my car was up on jacks."

He asked me about the horsepower, top speed, where I am from...all that stuff. Then he asked, "Do you always ride that fast?"

"Well, not always" I chuckled, "but when I'm out here in these open spaces, I like to do what I call recreational speeding."

"Oh, that's what you call it. Well, you've sure got the right bike for that kind of stuff."

Day, September 12, 2003
Day Sixteen: Arrive Saint George, Utah

"Yeah, I guess so," I answered. Then I added, "When you first walked over here, I thought maybe you were pissed because I passed you so fast."

"Nah, just curious about the bike," he said. "Good luck on your trip." After that, he walked back to his car and I saw him telling his wife about our conversation.

So, this was the way I was getting my kicks on the 1997 trip out west. My ultimate destination on that sojourn was San Francisco. There, I was to meet Kathy at the airport and together, we were to motorcycle up the coastal highway to Washington.

However, just north of Bishop on Route 120, everything changed when I wiped out the side of my bike taking a turn too fast; I hit a sandy patch in the road. The next thing I knew, the bike and I were sliding across the asphalt. The road-rash burned through the flesh on my left ass-cheek and sanded off some bone on the outside of my left knee. Strangely, that did not bother me much; I was just sad because my bike was out of commission. From a house nearby, I called the Bishop, California Honda dealer 50 miles away for a tow and some repairs. I spent the afternoon and that evening in the Bishop hospital emergency room, then got a motel.

I called Kathy and told her what happened. That went okay; she was just glad I was still in one piece. However, I was now without a bike, our plans had to change a little. Instead of a motorcycle road-trip, we would be taking a car trip. She asked me if I could still make San Francisco by 4:30 tomorrow afternoon to meet her plane. "No problem," I told her, In retrospect, I often thought my better angels caused that small accident to prevent me from risking Kathy's and my life riding up the coastal highway on a motorcycle. My thrill-seeking, which I played down to Kathy, was over the top and I couldn't see it at the time. Back home, my riding buddies and I would routinely run our bikes up to 170 or higher on our early Sunday morning rides. My fastest top end run on this Blackbird was 188 mph. Getting up to 170 is quite fast but after that, acceleration slows dramatically and it gives you time

Day, *September 12, 2003*
Day Sixteen: Arrive Saint George, Utah

to think about the nasty consequences of wiping out at that speed. Scary, but also a rush.

Anyway, first thing in the morning I was on the phone looking for a car rental. Not that easy in a remote town like Bishop. The only rental was from the local Chrysler dealer. They agreed to give me unlimited mileage for one week at a reasonable rate. That sounded great... until I found out what the car was: a four-cylinder, 93 horsepower, 1989 Dodge K-car. You know, the little square cars that were almost always white and looked like a refrigerator? Most of them were driven by old ladies with flowers attached to the radio antennas. It was all I could get and it ran okay, so I jumped in and I took off for San Francisco. It was 10AM. I had a full tank of gas, the weather was good and I had a timed mission: Get Kathy!

I got back on Route 120, passing by my crash site from the day before, and headed west through Yosemite National Park. I had exactly six-and-a-half hours to make it to San Francisco, a distance of 296 miles. That seemed doable, but I had to go through Yosemite National Park packed with RV's and sightseers. I hoped I wouldn't get bogged down in Bay area traffic, or get lost, which was very likely in an unfamiliar city. It still had not occurred to me that I was pushing my luck and taking too many risks. It was like something inside me was not working right. Since I had been riding like this, or crazier, for several years, I didn't give it much thought.

When I hit Yosemite, I knew I had to make time due to all the slow, sightseeing traffic, but it was going to be hard with this 93 horsepower, old ladies car and a very sore and heavily bandaged left ass-cheek and knee. I'll just drive smart, I reasoned. Passing other vehicles would require more forethought and planning. I couldn't pass anyone going uphill, that was out of the question. I could only pass on level and downhill roads.

On level ground, it was just a matter of flooring the gas peddle, passing and squeezing back into the line of traffic. Downhill was more challenging. I would gain momentum heading downhill, into a turn while

Friday, September 12, 2003
Day Sixteen: Arrive Saint George, Utah

scoping out the oncoming traffic after the turn. If it looked clear and the turn wasn't too tight, I could usually keep it floored through the turns and then pass as many cars and RVs as I could until I saw on-coming traffic, then I would squeeze back into my own lane. I did this all the way through Yosemite, which incidentally, is an incredibly beautiful place if you have time to look, which I did not.

Several cars tried to keep up; they were all young males. The two I remember best were a Mazda Miata, two-seater. He did not like getting passed by my little white refrigerator and took it very personally, staying on my tail. He tried to pass me back several times, finally fading into the background. The other was a young fellow in a yellow Mustang 5.0. He seemed very surprised I passed his little muscle car. Several times, he pulled up beside me, attempting to pass, then backed off for oncoming traffic. Thankfully, I did not cause an accident and made it to the San Francisco Airport an hour late due to heavy traffic and because I got lost in the city.

Nevertheless, Kathy and I were happy to see each other. The ride up the coastal highway to Seattle, Washington was not as exciting as it would have been on the bike, but it was safer and I loved traveling with Kathy. We had a wonderful time together.

When I returned to Bishop a week later to pick up my Blackbird, it felt like I was picking up my best friend from the hospital. It was great to be back in the saddle again. My ass and knee were still covered with gauze, but the injuries were healing. I headed east thinking I would take my time going home...no rush. After two days, I was in Flagstaff, Arizona where I bedded down for the night. That's when the idea hit me of seeing just how fast I could make it home to South Florida. The next morning, I was on the road at 7:30AM. I ate breakfast and headed east on I-40. I made 874 miles in thirteen hours. That night, at 7:30PM, I stopped at a motel a bit east of Oklahoma City near a town called El Reno.

The next morning, I stopped for a tasty breakfast-burrito with a side of home fries in a little Mexican restaurant not far away and at ten

Friday, September 12, 2003
Day Sixteen: Arrive Saint George, Utah

minutes after eight, I headed east to pick up I-35 which heads south to Dallas. In Dallas, I picked up I-20 east. So far, I had escaped all attempts at speeding tickets. Convinced I was now a bullet-proof speeder, I spotted a flashing blue light in my rear-view mirror. I got my first ticket just a few miles east of Dallas for speeding through midday traffic at 97 mph on I-20. Shortly after leaving Oklahoma City, I had decided I was going to make it home non-stop. So, when the cop was giving me the ticket, I was polite. But, it felt more like an interruption. I was a man on a mission

I stuffed the ticket in my pocket and as soon as the cop was out of sight, I was back at the one-hundred mark. At Shreveport, Louisiana, I took I-49, which heads southeast to I-10. I hit a lot of rain in Louisiana and had to stop under overpasses to put on my rain suit. Then, when the rain cleared, I had to
stop again to take it off...a real time waster. After the rain, I made a quick stop at Subway for a veggie-sub on whole wheat, then I hit I-10 east.

By the time I hit Florida, it was dark. On a motorcycle at night, I-10 through the Florida Panhandle is one weird ride, because I-10 travels through hundreds of miles of what is basically a tall pine forest. There is no highway lighting. The trees, close to the road on both sides, are insanely high
and the median strip is sometimes more than a hundred feet wide, populated with the same tall pines. Late at night, through this corridor of tall pine trees, in many places, even the moonlight was blocked out. Frequently the only light was my single, motorcycle headlight and the overall effect was like driving through a big, dark tunnel with spooky monster-shadows dancing on the walls. Want to look out for stray animals? Forget about it; it was way too dark.

Around midnight, one of the few cars on the road, traveling in my direction, was a white Camaro. I was doing 110 mph and he passed me. That got my adrenaline going and I caught him and passed him back. Then a while later, he passed me again. After that, I figured...okay, if

Friday, September 12, 2003
Day Sixteen: Arrive Saint George, Utah

you insist. I'll stay in back of you and you can hit the deer for me, no problem.

When I approached the entrance of the Florida State Turnpike heading south, I felt a great sense of relief. Now I had highway lighting and gas stations. I came within an inch of running out of gas on the panhandle, and everything closed at midnight. If I had not been carrying a 1.2-gallon emergency gas container, I would never have made it to Tallahassee where gas stations were open. I would have been out of luck. The next morning at 7:54AM, I pulled into my driveway. From the Mexican restaurant where I ate breakfast near Oklahoma City, I completed 1,524 miles in 23 hours and 54 minutes.

That trip flushed out a lot of my enthusiasm for motorcycles. I say this because, in the thirty-nine months before that trip, I rode a little over 90,000 motorcycle miles on six motorcycles I had bought during the same period. When I parked the bike in my garage after I came home, I didn't ride it again for six weeks. And even after that, I only rode an average of five-hundred miles a year for the next six years. My riding buddies fell by the wayside because I didn't call them. My subscriptions to various motorcycle magazines lapsed. I just lost interest in motorcycles.

After everything settled into my mind, I think I viewed that 1997 trip as my last hurrah. Reasoning, if I didn't kill myself after that trip, maybe I should consider myself lucky and cool it--- at least for a while. Besides, riding in Florida is very dull, no hills, no curvy roads, just traffic and flat, straight roads.

Back to my present 2003 trip, I had been thinking about this trip for some time. After almost six years, the idea of another motorcycle road-trip kept invading my mind. I kept putting it aside, mainly because I thought I would probably kill myself in some stupid accident. Why press my luck?

Anyway, my next destination is called The Little Ali-Inn. That's a play on the words, "little alien," as in space alien. I'm back on Route 6, which takes me to Nevada's Route 375. Because traffic is sparse, the

Friday, September 12, 2003
Day Sixteen: Arrive Saint George, Utah

speed limit is 75 mph, but I set my own pace. Route 375 is affectionately known as the "Extraterrestrial Highway." There are official Nevada State road signs at both ends of this highway that say EXTRATERRESTRIAL HIGHWAY in big, bold, white letters on a green background. The name resulted from all the UFOs that have been spotted here due to its proximity to "AREA 51," the secret US Government testing facility that for many years was so hush-hush, it officially didn't exist.

The EXTRATERRESTRIAL HIGHWAY runs right through Rachel, Nevada, with a population of about fifty people. The town consists of a mobile home park, gas station and the famous, bar-restaurant and UFO souvenir shop named "Little Ali-Inn." This place became famous, in part, because CBS's 60 Minute*s* featured it in connection with a segment on Area 51. Yes, people still see strange lights in the sky around the facility. These strange aircraft perform aerial maneuvers that are impossible for conventional aircraft. And, it all happens right around this US government airbase that didn't officially exist until recently.

The rumors, mostly from former civilian employees of Area 51, claim that these advanced crafts are really alien UFOs that crashed and were then retrieved by our government. Now we are trying to learn how they operate by test flying them over Area 51. The technology, so the stories go, is so advanced that these machines are, to us, like a modern computer would be to a scientist in the 19th century. At this point, we know how to push buttons to operate some features, but we can't reverse engineer the technology. It's just too advanced, although some people do claim we have learned a lot from studying these things.

I stopped at the Little Ali-Inn in 1997 and stayed over for two nights in a trailer used as a motel room. While drinking a few beers in the bar, I met a fellow about thirty-five, an Air Force Captain. He lived in the mobile-home park and worked, believe it or not, at Area 51, maintaining their computers. The captain offered to take me to the top of a small mountain and show me the actual, Area 51 facility first-hand. He

F*riday, September 12,*
Day Sixteen: Arrive Saint George, Utah

charged me 100 bucks, which I thought was a fair deal because it would take most of the day.

Around 9AM, we met at his trailer. Now that was a sight. He lived in a 40-foot trailer packed with computers and electronic gear. He had cleared only enough room to eat and a place to sit and watch TV. Everything else was electronics. He told me some of the stuff they work on at the base had to do with advanced aviation propulsion systems. He talked about a propulsion system that would allow fighter planes to travel more than 5,000 mph. This new propulsion system was called pulse-jet technology.

We took off in his pickup truck and headed up a mountain path on a dirt road. Eventually, the trail ended and we had to walk from there. After a two-hour hike, we arrived at the Area 51 lookout point. He set up his telescope tripod so we could see the facility. What I saw was utterly unremarkable. It was just airstrips, buildings that looked like concrete bunkers, airplane hangars and other structures that looked like, well, plain old two-story office buildings. "Most of the really neat stuff is underground or well hidden," he told me.

However, he did show me something interesting. He trained his telescope at a particular point in the distant forest and he said, "Here, look at this," pointing to the eyepiece. Hidden among the distant trees, I saw a surveillance camera and special, ultra-sensitive sound detection equipment designed to pick up on intruders. "It's all around the base," he told me. I, of course, wondered if we were under surveillance, but he told me the hill we were on was outside the restricted area and not to worry. Otherwise, he wouldn't be here himself. That evening when we returned, I met another interesting guy drinking at the Little Ali-Inn bar. He introduced himself as Richard from San Francisco and said he flew out to Las Vegas, about 90 miles south of Rachel, and rented a car to come out here and look for UFOs.

Over a couple of beers, he told me that he and his wife used to travel all over the world together. He had a consulting business based in San Francisco and dealt with several multinational corporations. They

Friday, September 12, 2003
Day Sixteen: Arrive Saint George, Utah

had a wonderful life together and were married for over thirty years. Then a few years ago, she
died of cancer. "When that happened," he said, "I went into a state of depression and started drinking pretty heavily. I'm an alcoholic," he candidly stated. "...a functioning alcoholic, but an alcoholic, nevertheless. I tried AA and stopped for a while." Then, he told me, "I understand my problem, but right now, I don't really want a solution." He was fascinated by the UFO thing and had read about the phenomena extensively, just as I have.

I've read dozens of books since I was a kid. The first UFO book I read was in 1955; UFOs are Real, written in 1950 by Major Donald Keyhoe, a former Navy pilot, a few years after the first modern-day UFO sighting in June 1947. After the 1947 sighting, there was a rush of sightings and, for many years, UFOs were making the front pages of newspapers and magazines. As an experienced pilot and graduate of the U.S. Naval Academy, Keyhoe was skeptical of all the UFO reports. However, True Magazine asked him to investigate the reports and write an article for their magazine. So, in 1949, he interviewed dozens of fliers as well as military officers in the Pentagon. To his surprise, he discovered that many of these aviation experts had seen the unexplained discs. Not only that, many of the pilots had seen them at close range.

After these interviews, his article "Flying Saucers Are Real" appeared in the January 1950 issue of True Magazine. It was a sensational article and soon after that, he wrote a book by the same title. After that first book, he wrote several more. As a 14-year old kid, UFOs are Real, was the one that got me started. I thought, my god if this is true it could change the world!

A few years ago, my wife and I actually saw a UFO fly over our house. No, we weren't drunk or on drugs. What happened, you ask? Well, early one evening before dark we were sitting on the back patio with our glasses of wine (our first one for the evening). I have no idea why, but I looked up at the sky. "Kathy, look at this," I said casually, as

Friday, September 12, 2003
Day Sixteen: Arrive Saint George, Utah

though I see these things all the time. Kathy looked up as this thing flew over our backyard, very low. It was about 1,000 feet above our heads and it was big. It was looked like a 727 airliner, except it didn't have any front wings, rear wings or tail rudder. It was metallic with window portals similar to an airliner, and it didn't make a sound as it slowly passed over us.

"What the fuck was that?" I asked Kathy. We looked at each other in amazement wondering, did we really see that? I swear, I could almost see through its windows; I couldn't, but that's how close it felt. It looked like it could have been conducting a tour of our little human community for a group of alien real estate developers. We never reported the sighting, because it was just our own personal experience and I really didn't care about it beyond that. I did do a little research on sightings of these tubular, wingless craft with portals, and discovered that other people have reported them over the years. So, we weren't alone on this type of sighting.

Former astronaut Gordon Cooper has told his UFO story a few times. He was one of the original Mercury Astronauts and the last American to fly in space solo. On May 15, 1963, he shot into space in a Mercury capsule for a 22-orbit journey around the world. During the final orbit, over Perth, Australia, he saw a glowing, greenish object ahead of him. He said it quickly approached his capsule. "It was real and it was solid. I know, because it was picked up by tracking radar, near Perth, Australia," he said.

John E. Mack, M.D., professor of psychiatry at Harvard Medical School worked with UFO abduction victims. He said that after interviewing hundreds of these victims, putting them under hypnosis and correlating their stories for consistency and information that could not have been shared among the abductees, he believed the abduction phenomena was real. He wrote several books on the subject and received heavy criticism from his Harvard colleagues and his bosses for his research on this subject, but he never changed his opinion.

Friday, September 12, 2003
Day Sixteen: Arrive Saint George, Utah

    Other people from academia have researched UFOs, and the abduction phenomena too. Moreover, once they seriously studied this UFO thing, they all came to the same general conclusion; these things are real. People are being taken up into these crafts and being examined and experimented on. Many experiments involve pregnancies where the babies are removed early in the gestation period, leaving a woman and her OB-GYN at a total loss as to what happened. Of course, all these stories are fascinating, but in the end, we don't know the answers to these two critical questions: Where did they come from, and why are they here?

    After sitting at the bar, drinking and sharing UFO stories with Richard for most of the evening, we each bought a six-pack of beer, put them on ice in the trunk of his rental car and around midnight, drove out into the desert to look for UFOs. The best viewing time is after 11PM. We drove southwest on the extraterrestrial highway for a few miles and turned right at the white landmark mailbox. The mailbox had become a landmark because it's the beginning of the not-so-secret, dirt road out to the Area 51 UFO viewing site.

    We made the right turn and headed out into the desert on a very dark gravel road for what seemed like forever. Eventually, we came to a sign that said: KEEP OUT – RESTRICTED U.S. GOVERNMENT AREA - USE OF DEADLY FORCE AUTHORIZED. We chuckled at the sign but didn't go past it. Once parked, we opened the trunk, pulled out two beers and started watching the night sky. A few minutes later—no UFOs, but we did spot what appeared to be an off-road vehicle, like a Jeep Wagon. The driver was shining his headlights at us. He was parked right on the other side of the threatening, KEEP OUT sign about 50-feet away.

    We tried to ignore him because we were warned that the security vehicles would try to intimidate us into leaving. So, we drank our beer and peed on the sagebrush until about 2AM. Still, no UFOs. Well, we tried. Now we were getting tired. We decided to call it a night. After a few wrong turns, due to our beer impaired-memories, we found our way

Friday, September 12, 2003
Day Sixteen: Arrive Saint George, Utah

back to the white mailbox and headed for the trailer park to get some sleep. I wish we could have gotten lucky, but it just wasn't our time.

Back to the present. Up ahead, I see the green and white highway sign "EXTRATERRESTRIAL HIGHWAY" and head for The Little Ali-Inn for a cold beer and time to cool off from the desert heat. The inside of this place is like a cheap, one-room restaurant. A long Formica counter-top bar is on my right as I walk in, and six or seven, square, Formica-top tables with chairs are to my left for diners. In the back are souvenirs: T-shirts with UFOs are Real and The Little Ali-Inn printed across the front. There are shelves stuffed full of UFO trinkets and books. On the walls are pictures of UFOs, mostly taken around Area 51.

While I'm sitting at the bar drinking a Heineken, a slim guy, about thirty-five, walks in the door wearing an expensive, all-weather, armored, full-body motorcycle outfit. If he had his full-face helmet on, he would look like someone in a space-suit. He sits down two stools to my right. I look past him and out the window to see what he's riding; it's a Suzuki Hayabusa. Now, this is a cool bike because it's currently considered the fastest production bike in the world with a top speed of 190 mph right off the showroom floor.

I introduce myself and ask him what he's doing out here. "I'm on a Motorcycle tour of Utah, Nevada and Southern California with a group from the American Motorcycle Association," he says, adding, "my group stopped in Las Vegas, but rather than hang around the hotel and gamble, I wanted to visit this famous Extraterrestrial highway and the Little Ali-Inn." He goes on to tell me he lives in Santa Cruz, California and works in Silicon Valley in the computer industry. After we finish our drinks, we step outside to talk and look at his new bike. His bike is clean; I mean spotless. It seems like it just came off the showroom floor. Plus, he has a very cool looking GPS device attached to his instrument cluster. I look at my bike. I have a $4.95 magnetic compass stuck on top of my speedometer with a rubber suction cup and every insect I've hit since I started my trip is still Stuck to my windscreen.

Friday, September 12, 2003
Day Sixteen: Arrive Saint George, Utah

    He asks me to take his picture in front of the Inn with his digital camera. Then I fished my flash camera from my tank bag and he takes my picture. It's all very nice. After the techy guy leaves, I ride down the street to the only gas station in Rachel, Nevada. The attendant is sitting inside his tiny cubical, noisy from the portable AC unit jammed into the window. He's busy watching his dog sleep on the floor. After gassing up my bike, I take off in the same direction as the Hayabusa.

    A few minutes later, I catch him and pull alongside. Sure enough, according to my speedometer, he's doing 75 mph out here in the middle of nowhere on his 190 mph motorcycle. Amazing self-restraint. Riding on Nevada desert roads makes me feel like I'm the only person on the planet. It's eerie. I can go 10 minutes sometimes and not pass another car; I know because I timed it more than once just to see if it was my imagination. Need to take a leak, no problem. If you like, just stop and pee right in the middle of the road. I did that too, just for the experience.

    From Route 375, I take Route 93 to Panaca, Nevada, a little town just west of Utah's state line. That's where I pick up Route 319 for a few miles and then cross over into Utah. For the next 40 miles, the roads are enjoyable with newly paved blacktop, gentle curves and changes in elevation. The landscape is endlessly beautiful red clay with natural formations etched into the mountain scenery. Next, I turn on to Route 56, which then runs into Route 18, which takes me to St George, Utah. St George is kind of a tourist town but very clean and pretty. It's nestled at the foot of several colorful plateaus and other natural earth formations, some of which look like a giant penis.

    I wonder if the religious groups had ever tried to outlaw these giant penis formations? Some of the phallic symbols look like they have a bad case of venereal warts too. Maybe it's just the way I see them, but I seriously doubt it. St. George is just a little south of Zion National Park, with Bryce Canyon a little to the northeast of that. I want to see both places tomorrow, so I stop here for the evening. Probably the same reason a lot of other tourists stay here. Poncho and Lefty's is a neat little Mexican restaurant, not far from my motel, so I eat dinner there.

Friday, September 12, 2003
Day Sixteen: Arrive Saint George, Utah

The song, made famous by Willie Nelson and Merle Haggard, tells the story of a Mexican bandit named Pancho, a revolutionary, and his questionable compadre, Lefty. It seems Lefty may have been paid-off by the Mexican Federales in exchange for Poncho's whereabouts. Lefty then heads north to the US, never to be heard of again and Poncho dies at the hands of the federales. "Poncho and Lefty" is a song I never get tired of listening to.

I like Mexican restaurants and the food here is good. I'm also able to get my daily fix of Heineken. However, I notice the Heineken beer label is different. It says, "This beer contains 3.2% alcohol or less by volume." That's a bit lower than usual; I guess that's a sign I'm in Utah. Frankly, I can't tell the difference. I love this restaurant and the food, but no luck engaging in conversations at the bar. I call it a night, talk with Kathy, shower and update my journal.

Saturday, September 13, 2003
Day Seventeen: Arrive Escalante, Utah

I overslept, but it feels good and I'm invigorated. After my usual Denny's breakfast, I'm on the road again with beautiful weather. Onto I-15 North, then an exit to Route 12 and onto Route 9, which leads me right through Zion National Park. Zion is an ancient Hebrew word meaning, "a place of refuge or sanctuary." The park is a beautifully scenic eight-mile ride full of hilly, striking, red-clay rock formations that showcase the natural beauty of Utah.

I make a couple of short stops to stretch and take in the awesome beauty. My next stop is Bryce Canyon. Bryce Canyon is a breath-taker. Traffic is slow and the narrow two-lane road is full of RVs, cars and motorcycles. I don't mind because I want to savor the sights. I can't help taking pictures. I know I'm taking too many, but each vista point is more scenic than the last. The brochure I got at the entrance gate says Mule Deer, Golden Eagles and Mountain Lions inhabit the park. I didn't see any, so I have to take their word on that. What I do know for sure is that it's cold, mainly because of the elevation which runs between eight-thousand and nine-thousand-feet.

Bryce Canyon was created as a national park in 1928. When the early Mormon settlers came to the area, a homesteader, named Ebenezer Bryce, built his home in here where the park's lodge stands today. His neighbors started referring to the area as Bryce's canyon, and the name stuck. Later, when Bryce was asked about his thoughts on the canyon, he replied, "It's a heck of a place to lose a cow."

It's a Saturday and the place is busy with backpacking hikers, tent campers and bicyclists. Utah attracts the outdoorsy type and it's easy to see why with so much natural beauty and a great selection of national parks.

After Bryce, I get back on Route 12 and head west. This is one of those days motorcyclists dream about. The weather is cool, the sky is clear, sunny with beautiful scenery and hundreds of miles of twisty, curvy blacktop straight ahead. On top of all that, the bike sounds great and responds eagerly to my throttle commands.

Friday, September 12, 2003
Day Sixteen: Arrive Saint George, Utah

There are two kinds of mountain drivers: The ones that do just fine, they probably live in the west, or they're just good drivers; or the kind who fear mountain roads. They're convinced that given half a chance, their car will speed out of control and bolt from the road, charging over a cliff taking them and their passengers to a fiery death, thousands of feet below. They drive with a death-grip on the wheel and they're constantly riding the brake pedal. I've seen them pulled off to the side of the road with their front brakes actually on fire. It's this latter group that you don't want driving in front of you on the mountains. They will drive you crazy. You have to pass them, double lines or no double lines.

So, that's what I do; I have fun screaming by them, heading into the next curve. I have patience when I'm behind a sensible driver maintaining a brisk pace. However, on a fast bike, it's so easy to just zip around these slowpokes, there isn't much need to wait. Passing cars and RVs in the mountains is actually part of the enjoyment, I think. After a fun ride through the curvy highland roads, I enter Escalante, Utah and check into a motel for the night. This is a small town, maybe a few thousand residents in southern Utah. The area was settled in 1875. The town is named after a Spanish Missionary, Father Silvestre Velez de Escalante, who traveled near the Escalante River on an expedition in 1776. They get a little tourist business but you can tell it's not a tourist town in the normal sense, mostly

Campers, hikers and other outdoor types. I throw my luggage in the room and ride about a quarter-mile down the road until I spot a cozy-looking pizza restaurant with an open, second-story wood deck patio facing the street. It has a breathtaking view of the nearby mountains. The sun is starting to set and the scenery borders on spiritual. After ordering a beer and a veggie pizza with no cheese, I relax and let the afternoon sun warm my body. My god, this is great! Hungrier than I expected, I quickly devour

Saturday, September 13, 2003
Day Seventeen: Arrive Escalante, Utah

my pizza and another beer. Content now with a full belly and a small glow from the beers, I order my third beer because I don't want to leave this place. I just want to sit here in the warmth of the setting sun and enjoy the experience.

My mind drifts to Kathy and how she influenced me to adopt a vegan diet in the 1980s. "It's better for our health, the animals and the environment," she told me and gave me a couple of books to read. She was always ahead of the curve on food, our daughter's education and the discipline of regular exercise. But more importantly, she just has a kind heart. I get like this when I'm homesick for Kathy. I don't know if I'll make it for 30 days.

A few minutes go by and the waitress comes out to see how I'm doing. I'm the only customer right now, so we talk a little. I ask her about the liquor laws in Utah because I had heard they were different, and I noticed the 3.2% alcohol content on the beer labels. "People don't have any problem getting served liquor or beer in Utah," she tells me. "The problems really rest with the restaurants and bars, because Utah has such complicated licensing requirements. For example," she goes on, "it's okay to have a regular beer bar, but only if you serve microbrew beers from Utah. If you're serving national, brand-name beers you can only serve the beer to diners at their tables in a restaurant setting."

"So, they only want stand-alone beer-bars to serve beer made in Utah," I answer, restating the obvious.

"That's about it." She smiles, then goes on to say, "In the beginning, Utah was basically dry because of the Mormon influence. Later, politicians started making more and more exceptions, mainly to encourage tourism. Eventually, they made so many convoluted exceptions and re-interpretations of the old laws, they wound up with a set of liquor licensing laws that look more like the US tax code; way too complicated." She looks to be in her mid-20s. Curious about why someone her age lives here, I ask her how she got to this little town. "I followed my parents out here," she says. "They owned a vacation home here and then retired and moved here full-time. I really like it here now,"

Saturday, September 13, 2003
Day Seventeen: Arrive Escalante, Utah

she tells me with a big smile. Then she proudly adds, "In fact, I just bought my own home here, so I guess I'll be here for a while."

Then she tells me, "My friends from Vermont, where I came from, always ask me, 'what the hell do you do there in the middle of nowhere? Where do you shop? There isn't even a Walmart.'" Then she laughs, saying, "Vacationers here at the restaurant ask me the same thing. But you know what?" She smiles. "I tell them, it's not a problem, I couldn't imagine living anywhere else, we have four restaurants, one small grocery store and I hang out with my friends. We just hang out at each other's house, that's all."

Listening to her story, I'm wondering, could I do this? Could I live in a small western town with great places to ride my motorcycle, gobs of natural beauty, no traffic problems, and cheap houses? I think I would love it, but I doubt if I could sell it to Kathy, not just yet. We live only a few blocks for our daughter, her husband and our two grand-kids. It would kill Kathy to be separated from them. Our conversation ends when another couple sits down to eat. "Great view, don't you think?" I ask, looking in their direction.

"Oh yes, we agree. That's why we're here." They're from Colorado. The wife tells me they've lived there for twenty years. "We like to drive over here for the beautiful sights and to do some hiking," she adds.

After I tell them I'm from Florida, she says, "Oh, we lived in Orlando, Florida for many years, but now we wouldn't think of moving back to Florida. Not yet anyway, not until we get too old for hiking and skiing." His wife looks at her husband and smiles in agreement.

Who knows, maybe Kathy will come around some and I'll get my chance. I'm missing her more every day now. I don't know how much more touring I'll want to do after I see Utah. I certainly want to check out Arches National Park, Kathy read about it before I left and said it is amazing to see. I also want to visit the Mormon Center in Salt Lake City

Sunday, September 14, 2003
Day Eighteen: Arrive Moab, Utah

I don't have an alarm and it doesn't matter what time I get up. Last night, I went to bed at 9PM. I got ten hours of sleep. Could I have been that tired? I love it when I get a shower that has a strong flow of warm water shooting out. Not this morning though, more like an old fart with a swollen prostate trying to take a leak, the water just dribbles out. I check my chain for looseness every morning now. It seems like every two days I have to tighten it. Today is the second day. It was a close call, so I decide to let it ride for another day.

My breakfast is shitty. I have plain oatmeal because they have no fruit and no raisins. Nothing to put on the oatmeal. I order hash browns and they're okay. The waitress agrees to leave off the butter and bring me some catsup, but not without giving me the impression that I'm a pain in her ass.

Several Harley riders are eating near my table. They are mostly dressed in Black leather. The men wear leather chaps and the women wear leather jackets with lots of fringe hanging off the arms and across the back. Reminds me of when Kathy and I had our '94 Harley Softail Custom, we had a lot of fun on that Harley. We enjoyed hanging out with other Harley riders. It got old though after a while. I began to feel more at home on my lighter, faster and better handling sport-bikes. So, the Harley just sat in my garage until one day, I realized that phase was over and I sold the Harley. No regrets, just great memories.

At 9AM, I say goodbye to Escalade and head north on Route 12 to Route 24 west. In Hanksville, I have to decide if I'm going to do the southern loop on Route 95 or head north on 24. My objective, in either case, is to wind up at Arches National Park. I have plenty of time and according to the computer guy on the Hayabusa, the southern loop on Route 95 is a scenic, one day ride of about 400 miles. I decide to take the Route 95, southern loop. That will take me within about 30 miles from the Northern Arizona state-line. At which point, I loop and come back north on Route 191. That brings me within roughly 30-miles from "Four-Corners," the point where Utah, Arizona, Colorado and New

Saturday, September 13, 2003
Day Eighteen: Arrive Moab, Utah

Mexico meet. From here, I'll head north up to Moab where I'll visit Arches National Park.

The Hayabusa rider was right, some of this scenery is too beautiful to describe. However, one thing I can describe is the temperature, at times is colder than the inside of a Sub-Zero Freezer. The scenery is expansive, and red clay foothills, plateaus and other oddball formations dominate the landscape. I take a lot of pictures and when I stop for gas, I buy a little book with professional quality photos. The roads are fun, with both tight twisty turns, long sweeping curves and long straight two-lane roads. Everything a motorcyclist could hope for.

Once, while I was cruising along, taking in the sights, a guy on a big Goldwing with his lady on the back passed me like I was an old geyser in a 1952 Plymouth. But I'm enjoying the scenery. There's just too much to see. I want to go slow right now and enjoy the sights. Later in the day, I speed up and have some fun with the curves. I play a game of trying to judge my fastest entry speed into a curve without using the brakes. In the west, at least in certain parts, there are a lot of road signs warning for cattle, deer and wildlife on the roads. I've seen lots of cattle grazing right along the edge of the road on my trip, as well as deer. But the thing I see the most, all over the west, are skid marks that lead off the edge of the road. They're all over the place. I can only assume the drivers were breaking to avoid hitting a big animal.

I saw a group of deer the other day. One of them jumped over the retaining fence that ran along the road like it was just a mild inconvenience and started munching grass not six inches from the edge of the road. When I stopped to take a picture, he jumped back over the fence to join his friends. I've seen dozens of cattle grazing on the edge of the road. These animals pretty much go where they feel like.

Gassing up, I meet a guy that is riding my next motorcycle. It's a Yamaha FJR 1300, it puts out 145 horses, has an adjustable windscreen, ABS brakes and shaft-drive. So, I don't have to screw around with chain adjustments anymore…and it looks handsome. Maybe I'll get one for my next long trip. The guy that's riding it says it's very comfortable on a

Saturday, September 13, 2003
Day Eighteen: Arrive Moab, Utah

long ride. His wife is also riding a motorcycle, a smaller bike, suitable for her size. Lovely couple, they look to be in their fifties.

I find a motel in Moab, about three miles south of Arches Park, which I'll visit tomorrow morning. After dumping off my bags in the motel, I find a remarkable bar and restaurant that specializes in microbrewery beers. Inside, the place has an expansive, open feel with lots of wood and high windows to capture the sunlight and scenic views…a great atmosphere. They even have several veggie entries on the menu, which excites me as much as the beer selection. Sitting at the bar, I order black bean soup with onions and some other neat stuff on it. Then I have a burrito with six or seven different veggies inside; I feel like I hit the veggie-dining jackpot.

While eating and drinking my microbrew beer, I talk with two other guys that were here for a little vacation. One guy, in his mid-50s, is driving a 31-foot motor home and wants to talk about politics. I'm not in the mood for that, so I just play along for a while. He's a diehard liberal like me, but my heart just isn't in it. Sometimes when you talk with people that have the same views, it's like talking into an echo chamber. Fortunately, this guy finishes his beer and leaves.

I start a conversation with a guy on my other side that looks to be in his thirties. He's a rock climber out here scaling vertical cliffs with a friend of his. Today, he lost his grip and fell 33 feet. His safety rope abruptly stopped his fall. "It really shook me up," he confesses, "because I bounced off a few rocks before I stopped and put a big gash in my leg just below my knee." He points to his bandaged leg. I ask him if he wore knee pads and a helmet. "Yeah, I did," he says, "but this one got me below the knee." I ask him if he is going back out tomorrow, and he says, "Yeah, that's the hardest part, to go back out tomorrow and finish the climb because, right now, I'm a little nervous."

One of the most insightful comments he makes about rock climbing is that it doesn't take a lot of raw strength. "Mostly what it takes," he says, "is a lot of nerve and the ability to stay cool under stress."

Saturday, September 13, 2003
Day Eighteen: Arrive Moab, Utah

"I believe you," I reply sincerely.

The rock climber finishes his beer and leaves. Another guy, a few feet away and around the corner of the bar, ask me where I'm from. I tell him I'm from South Florida on a motorcycle vacation. He looks about 30 and tells me he lives in Santa Cruz, California. "I work in Silicon Valley on computer software, at least I did until I got laid off because of a slowdown." I hear the resignation in his voice.

This guy reminds me of the computer guy on the 190 mph Hayabusa I met at the Little Ali-Inn. He also lives in Santa Cruz and works in Silicon Valley. This guy doesn't ride a Hayabusa; however, he drives a Volkswagen Passat. He says he loves it and since losing his job, he's been touring the western states sightseeing. "Eventually, my savings will run out and my unemployment compensation will stop, but in the meantime," he tells me, "I'm having fun. I just hope I have another job when the money runs out." He is very interested in motorcycles. He never really had any experience except as a passenger one time on his friend's small bike. But, he asks me a lot of questions about how the handling characteristics and dynamics of motorcycles differ from cars.

He's surprised to find out that you can't stop a motorcycle while it's in a turn. "Why is that?" He innocently asks.

"Well, the simple answer is, you will crash the bike," I say with a grin. "No, seriously, the bike needs momentum to stay leaned over while turning. Take away the momentum by braking and the bike falls over. So, to stop a motorcycle, two things must first occur: the bike has to be perpendicular to the road and the front wheel must be straight in line with the back wheel. In other words, the bike has to be in an upright position, moving in a straight line."

"I guess that's the nice thing about cars, you can stop them any old way you want," he smiles.

"True," I say, taking a sip of beer. "Another interesting thing about motorcycle dynamics," I continued, "when a motorcycle is going in a straight line and an object or animal appears directly in front of the

Saturday, September 13, 2003
Day Eighteen: Arrive Moab, Utah

bike unexpectedly, the motorcyclist has two choices, go around the object or brake. You can't do both at the same time or you'll crash."

He is fascinated by the difference in the physical dynamics of motorcycles versus cars. He'd never thought about this stuff. While we are talking, he's slicing up cloves of garlic and eating them with his beer. He says he is eating the garlic and taking massive doses of vitamin C because he doesn't want to catch a cold on his vacation. I'm thinking, this is one health-conscious guy. Then, he surprises me by going outside to smoke a cigarette. You never can tell.

Monday, September 15, 2003
Day Nineteen: Arrive Provo, Utah

I had this weird dream last night. While I'm on this trip, I cut my hair with my electric clippers. The problem is, I used the wrong attachment and before I realized what I was doing, I had created these big bald patches on the back side of my head. Now, I've got this big dilemma in my dream: should I go home early because I look so weird, or just say fuck it and keep on going while my hair grows back? A dream about my vanity. Oh, how the mind works.

I have to go out and adjust that goddamn chain again this morning…and it's cold! My hands are freezing. It makes me think of that guy from Massachusetts on the Suzuki 1100 that I met in the Sierra Mountains while we waited side by side at in traffic at a road construction site.
He said he ran into cold weather on his ride through North Dakota. "My hands got so cold I had to hold them under hot water for 30 minutes until they got back to normal," he told me.

Moab, this town I'm in now, has a Denny's so I figure I'll have another excellent breakfast this morning before my ride through Arches National Park. But, Denny's is a bust, I wait and wait for a seat. No luck. So, while I'm waiting, I look around. One of the waitresses is coughing and sneezing like she has a bad cold. And the place looks dirty like it's poorly managed. I think I should follow my instincts on this one and go somewhere else like I should have done the other night at the Mexican restaurant. My instincts were right that night, but I didn't listen.

So, I walk out just as the hostess arrives and ride back to my motel. As I reach my motel, I notice a cozy little café called, "The Jail House," because that's what it was many years ago. The place looks clean and comfortable so, I leave my bike at the motel and walk over.

My breakfast is outstanding: oatmeal with fresh fruit, dry English muffin with raspberry jam and hash-browns with my favorite catsup. I talk with a retired couple at the table next to me. They came from Texas and are traveling around the west in their RV on a three-week tour, just having a good time. The husband asks about my travel plans. I tell him I'm on a motorcycle vacation from Florida. That leads to a story about a bad accident he had 45 years ago on his Indian motorcycle.

Monday, September 15, 2003
Day Nineteen: Arrive Provo, Utah

He says it took him two years to recover, and then he tells me, "I never rode again." Knowing that most riders back then didn't wear helmets, I ask him if he had gotten any head injuries, "No, it was my leg, I broke it in six places." Then he says, "My son is into motorcycles, he works on them at a Kawasaki dealership where we live. He had a bad accident too, but unlike me, he still rides the damn things. He tells me, "Dad, how can I work on them and not ride them, I have to test-ride them after I do the work."

As they get up to leave, he says, "You be careful on your trip." Nice couple. So many people have motorcycle accident stories, someone should write a book. I pay my bill, get back on the bike and head for Arches National Park. The morning air is clear and chilly, so I stop and put on my jacket liner. Oh yeah, that feels good! This is one of the most beautiful parks in the world with over two thousand natural sandstone arches, including what's known as the world-famous, sixty-foot-tall freestanding natural arch known as, Delicate Arch. There's also cool looking balanced rocks that should have fallen over years ago, but they never do. The place is full of incredible red, orange and rust colors and textures so unique, only mother nature could think them up.

My first impression is, this looks like something from another planet. I take gobs of pictures. I even do two hikes off the main path to see the more spectacular arches, like the Delicate Arches I just mentioned. I'm not a hiker, but I can't resist these impressive sights. In all, I do about five miles of hiking, about half of it uphill. A lot of people on the hiking trails can't make it. But surprisingly, quite a few older people did the whole uphill walk. They were mostly from other countries though; in fact, Americans are in the minority. This has got to be a must-see place for foreign travelers when they visit the states.

On my hiking, I meet people from Asia, Germany, England, Denmark. You name it, they're here. It becomes easy to spot the foreigners on the climbing part of the hike because the fat Americans keep dropping behind or just giving up. In all, I spend about four hours in the park and could easily have spent the whole day. There are also a

Monday, September 15, 2003
Day Nineteen: Arrive Provo, Utah

lot of bicyclists. There are even trails for off-road vehicles. After Arches, I head north on Route 191 then I-70 West and again, north on Route 191, which leads to Route 6, which will land me in Provo, just south of Salt Lake City. From there, it's a short run on I-15 to the Great Mormon Tabernacle Church.

The ride from Arches to Provo is enjoyable with warm, clear weather and it's easy to cruise between 90 and 100 mph. As I get closer to Provo, I hit some mountains and it gets cold again. I stop and put on my jacket liner. Now I feel frisky. I have a little fun zipping past cars and trucks on the mountain roads. About a week ago, I bought a 1.2-gallon emergency gasoline container, filled it with gas and strapped it on the back of my bike. Today, I coast into Provo on fumes and come very close to needing that extra gas. Sure, it's reassuring having it there, just in case. That extra gas saved my ass during my 1997 trip and it may do it again.

By five o'clock, I am whipped—probably all the hiking earlier today, plus a little of the age thing. I know this though; my butt is hurting me and my right hand keeps falling asleep from leaning on it all day. I lean on both hands, but only the right one, my throttle hand, gets numb. So, I engage my throttle lock and shake my hand, then slap it against my thigh to bring it back to life. Next, I stand up on my foot pegs with a good grip on the handlebars. This puts my ass way up in the air and gives it a rest while I let the fresh air blow through my crotch, bringing my vital parts back to life.

People are looking at me from their cars, probably thinking I'm going to jump off my motorcycle. I'm daydreaming about buying the Yamaha FJR 1300 I saw yesterday when I was buying gas. It's comfortable, fast, has ABS brakes, adjustable windscreen and no chain to adjust or oil. What a great bike. It would solve all my problems. Now, this is weird, because just as I'm approaching Provo on I-15, I see a billboard advertisement for a Yamaha, motorcycle dealer. I think, maybe I should take a look. I don't have to actually buy one, I'll just check it

Monday, September 15, 2003
Day Nineteen: Arrive Provo, Utah

out. Well, I ask directions at a gas station and within ten minutes, I'm at the dealership.

I ask the salesman if they have any of the new Yamaha FJR 1300s in stock. He smiles at me like I am about eight years old and says, "No way, those things are sold before they hit the showroom floor." Then he tells me, "No one can get enough of them because it's a limited production model. We have to special order them."

"Well, I guess that settles that," I say. Then I ask him if he has a brochure I could take with me, which he kindly gives me. At least I can drool over the pictures until I get home. Right now, my body is telling me to find a motel and relax. I spot a Ramada Inn at the next exit off I-15. Fifty bucks a night. More than I like to spend, but I'm not in the mood to shop prices right now. Am I ever in the mood to shop prices?

I call Kathy; she's had a rough day. Listening to her unload conjures up guilt for leaving her alone so long. I tell her I love her and miss her, which is true. "I'm thinking about heading home; I'm getting homesick," I confess. She assures me everything is okay and I should enjoy myself. She doesn't think I should hurry home because it wouldn't do any good. "I'm doing just fine," she tells me sincerely. "I just needed to vent."

"Should I feel insecure that you don't need me," I tease, "Or just happy?"

"Happy," she chirps back. "Now enjoy your trip."

I know she is trying to make me feel better, but I want to hear her get excited that I might be coming home early, not encourage me to stay away longer. I mean, it's nice to feel wanted, you know what I mean? I want her to say, "I miss you baby and yes, please come home sooner!"

Then she says, "I do want you here, Kenny, but I also want you to finish your trip, you may never have another chance to do this. I don't want you to come home because you feel worried or guilty "Eddy and I are okay. I'm getting things done around the house and making my own decisions.

Monday, September 15, 2003
Day Nineteen: Arrive Provo, Utah

Look, I handled the work on the kitchen walls by myself and it turned out fine. Today, I was a little hassled. I guess I shouldn't have told you that because you'll worry."

"No-no, I want you to tell me what's on your mind. I love you, sweetie."

"I love you too, Kenny, just enjoy your trip. Okay?"

I'm still not entirely sure about how to feel. Still, I decide to take Kathy's advice and finish my trip, but first, I need to take a shower.

I try finding a place to eat, but all I see are fast food joints. Eventually, I come across a Mexican restaurant, but there are so many kids in the place it sounds noisier than a daycare center for preschoolers. So, I look at the hostess and say, "Nooo…I don't think so, too many children," and walk out.

I end up eating at an Italian fast food place. The food sucks. How bad is it? Well, it is so bad I return the bowl of soup to get back my $2.17 as an act of protest. Unfortunately, I do eat the spaghetti, which travels through my digestive system like an overdose of Ex-lax and an hour later, my intestinal tract is entirely flushed out. I figure I won't need to shit again for three days. After I recover from all that excitement, I go wash my clothes and finish the day with clean outerwear and clean innards. What a day!

Monday, September 15, 2003
Day Twenty: Arrive Richfield, Utah

The morning finds me eating the motel's continental breakfast because there aren't any restaurants around here worth eating in. I'm on the road at 9:30. Arriving in Salt Lake City. A gas station attendant tells me where to find the Mormon Center. After circling the area twice, looking for a secure parking area, I pull into a lot with a parking attendant at $5 per day. The parking lot attendant is a 79-year-old German guy and a certified motorcycle nut. He tells me about the two, old BMW bikes he has at his house. Then, he replays a couple of his favorite motorcycle stories for me. Finally, he says, "Park it right here," pointing at a spot next to the little gatehouse that he stands in. "And I'll watch the bike and your riding gear. I'll make sure nothing happens to it," he assures me. A sweet old guy.

The Mormon Center, also known as Temple Square, takes up a whole city block. Plus, there are other related facilities on the surrounding streets. For instance, on the next block is a huge building built as a memorial to Brigham Young. He wasn't the founder of the Mormon religion, that was Joseph Smith, but Young was more instrumental in molding the religion into what it is today. The building is a tribute to Young. It features a first-class restaurant, a library, lecture hall, and more. This section of town is very clean, the kind of area you wouldn't think twice about taking a walk late at night. They have all the name-brand shops, and trendy restaurants you see in other big cities. But here, everything just looks cleaner. Flowers are also a prominent part of the landscape around the Mormon facilities. A beautiful scene indeed.

My first stop is the Mormon Tabernacle. They have an organ recital every day at noon, and the public is welcome to listen to the majestic 12,000-pipe organ. There's no choir, just the organ. They use these striking lighting effects that cause the enormous organ pipes to change color depending on the mood they want to create in the Tabernacle. It's incredibly beautiful to see. I clap after the organist completes her first piece. No one else is clapping…I feel like a dork. Then at the end, everyone applauds, so I joined in too…I'm on the right track, just a little early.

Monday, September 15, 2003
Day Twenty: Arrive Richfield, Utah

No one is allowed in the actual Mormon Temple, I'm told, because it's a sacred place, only Mormons that are suitably educated in the religion and fully committed to Jesus and God are permitted to enter that building. So, yes, even some Mormons are excluded. I take a guided tour of the Mormon Welcome Center. It has elaborate displays of Jesus and other well-known biblical figures. The centerpiece of the Welcome Center is a perfect miniature model of the city of Jerusalem. Two girls, probably in their late teens and excellent speakers, lead the tour and take turns talking; they were well educated in their religion and plainly intelligent. It is interesting how comfortable they talk about the tenants of their religion. Not the least bit of doubt or hesitation in their voice. They speak as if everything were just a matter of fact, not faith.

Also, very noticeable—the place is full of tourists from foreign countries and many of the Mormon tour guides are from foreign countries as well: Japan, Taiwan, England, you name it. I ask one of our two guides about this and she says, "The young Mormons from foreign countries come here as part of their missionary program. Also, the church wants tourists to meet Mormons from their home countries so they relate better to the religion and it makes them aware that Mormonism is part of their home country's religious community."

One sweet Japanese girl, a former Buddhist says, "I incorporate some of my Buddhist beliefs into my Mormon religion." She goes on to say, very sincerely, "If you truly believe in the Mormon faith, it will change your life forever." I tell her, "I'm sure that's true for many people, But I could never commit to one religion." She just smiles at me like, 'You don't know what you're missing.'

After the Mormon tour, I spend the next half-hour walking around town trying to find the place where I parked my bike. Kathy would remember exactly where to go; she actually pays attention to things like this. It is 1:30PM now and I'm still not sure where I'm going next on my trip. I am pretty sure, however, that I want to generally head south and stay away from any cold weather farther north. So, I head for

Monday, September 15, 2003
Day Twenty: Arrive Richfield, Utah

Interstate 15 and stop at the first exit with a Denny's restaurant. I ate that light continental breakfast at the motel and now I'm starving.

While I'm eating a veggie burger, I call Kathy for help. Between the two of us, I decide to head south and ride along the southernmost border of Texas and see Big Bend National Park and some of the Texas border towns as I meander back to Florida …thanks, Kathy. Back on I-15, I hit heavy traffic until I am well south of Provo. About one-hundred miles south of Salt Lake City, I take Route 50 to get off the Interstate for a while. That brings me to I-70 South, and fifteen miles later, I'm in Richfield, Utah, a small town with some restaurants and motels, so I stop for the night.

The ride to Richfield is incredibly windy. The thing is, on a motorcycle, those wind gusts feel like 85 mph. At times, it seems like the bike is just going to blow off the road like a piece of scrap paper from a fast-food takeout. The best I can do is keep the bike within a four-foot-wide strip of the road. I zip past several 18-wheelers going in my direction. I am doing between 95 and 100 mph when I overtake those big mothers. As I blast past the front end of the trucks, the wind turbulence forces my bike to lean over like I am in the middle of a turn. I really can't recall anything like it. It is even worse in the open valleys between the low-lying mountain ranges south of Provo. I wonder, what do other people think about when they're riding motorcycles all day, fighting wind gusts, rain, cold weather, heavy traffic and scary mountain passes?

Here's what I think about: should I pass that car now? How fast can I enter this curve? Damn it's cold, but if I stop now to put on something warm, all those vehicles I just passed on this narrow two-lane mountain road will pass me. Then, I'll have to pass them all over again. Nah, I'll just freeze until I need gas. I wonder how strong the wind has to blow before my bike goes entirely off the road at 90 mph. Oh shit, open range territory again…got to keep my eye out for deer and cattle. Oh boy, a thunderstorm! I wonder how often lightning hits a motorcycle. And my personal favorite, FOG! This is what also makes motorcycle

Monday, September 15, 2003
Day Twenty: Arrive Richfield, Utah

touring an adventure. It's what makes the good days sublimely enjoyable. You can't get that stimulation in a car. Cars are boring, that's why so many people fall asleep at the wheel. They actually kill themselves from boredom.

It turns out the whole town of Richfield is infested with four-wheel ATVs (all-terrain vehicles with motorcycle engines.) They're all over the place running around like supercharged cockroaches, and they're noisy little fuckers too. It's hard to find a motel because of this ATV event that is going on. It is like Daytona Bike Week with ATVs. I finally locate a shit-hole motel for $26.95 and feel lucky about that because it could have been the last room in town for the night. The motel owner that checks me in is morbidly obese. It takes her, and I swear I'm not making this up, at least three minutes to get out of her living room chair and walk to the front desk of the motel office, a distance of about 15-feet.

I watch her slowly turn around with her walker and carefully back herself into the chair behind the counter. Feeling her pain, I can't help asking, "Is there anything I can do to help?" She replies very slowly and short of breath, "No, it…just…takes…a…little…time." It is painful to watch. Finally, she plops down in her chair with a big thud and breathes a sigh of relief. Next, she reaches for a registration form, then a pen and with thoughtful, deliberate strokes, she carefully constructs every letter of my name on top of the form.

I ask, "Would you like me to do that for you?"

She stops writing, and looks up to say, "No, that's ok, it's easier if I do it." Then she looks down again and continues the laborious task of copying the information from my license and credit card onto the registration form. She talks at about the same speed she writes, like a glacier. But eventually, I do get checked in. I ask her if there is a bar in town where I can get a beer.

She replies, again, very slowly, "There's only one bar in town called The Detour, it's a couple of blocks down the street." I thank her, wondering how she'd get back to her living room.

Monday, September 15, 2003
Day Twenty: Arrive Richfield, Utah

The bar is dark and old. Looking around, it appears everyone is drinking Bud or Miller. I order a miller. The guy sitting next to me is a friendly sort and we strike up a conversation. He tells me he grew up in this town. Then, for twenty years he worked and lived in Salt Lake City doing construction work so he could make enough money to take care of his sick father. "Three years ago, my dad died...he was 91. I've been living here ever since."

I ask him how old he is, thinking he'd say maybe 68 or something like that. "I'm 48," he tells me. Damn, I think to myself, this guy's had one hard life. He's missing both front teeth and his skin looks like aged leather. Taking a drag of his cigarette, he says he loves ATVs and proudly tells me that in the last two years, he's only missed two weekends of riding his ATV.

As we are talking, his buddies are looking at a big ATV trail map spread out over a pool table in back of us. They're trying to figure out the best trails for tomorrow's ride. Apparently, this is the place to live if you're an ATV enthusiast. I drink another beer, talk with the barmaid and play a few songs on the jukebox, then leave to find a place to eat dinner.

I find a little Mexican restaurant down the street. A young, perky, blond hostess comes over, hands me a menu and asks me if I am in town with the ATV group. "No," I say, "I'm just passing through." She could see I was carrying my motorcycle helmet, so I add, "I'm on a motorcycle vacation."

A few minutes later, the waitress comes over. She's also very cute with straight blond hair. She looks like a high school cheerleader and asks me if I'd like to know the specials. I say, "No, not really...I think I know what I want, but first, can I get a beer?"

"Oh no," she says, "We don't serve beer."

"Well, I'll just have a glass of water then."

"Are you sure you don't want a coke or something?"

"No" I assure her, "The water's just fine." Then I ask her for a vegetarian burrito.

Tuesday, September 16, 2003
Day Twenty: Arrive Richfield, Utah

She looks at me with a blank stare and says, "What's that?"

"Look," I tell her, appealing to her maternal instincts, "The thing is, I'm a vegetarian. Maybe you can help me figure out something that I can eat." She smiles warmly, as though she likes the idea of helping a lone vegetarian lost in the middle of meat-eating country. Together, we decide how to word the order for the cook, who may never have met an actual vegetarian. She even takes special effort to make sure the cook doesn't use cheese. I tell her, "Cooks aren't used to making these things without cheese."

"Oh, don't worry, I'll make sure." She smiles like she's really going to watch over the whole thing. She is delightfully sweet about it.

Then she tells the other blond, "He's a vegetarian," as they both look over at my table like I was a visitor from Mars. Then together, they head back to the kitchen and explain the whole thing to the cook. Now, I see all three of them, looking at my table. I'm beginning to feel very important now, like a VIP customer. I decide to go take a leak in the men's room. I'm gone maybe three minutes. When I return, the whole meal, burrito, with a side of rice and beans is sitting on my table, steaming hot and ready to eat. Not only that, it's a burrito just like I ordered and it is delicious. I devour it like a hungry dog and raise my hand for the cute little waitress.

She asks, "Is everything okay?"

She had already been to my table once to check on me, so I say, "Yeah, this is great!" This bought me another big smile. Then I say, "I'd like to order another whole meal, is that okay?"

"Yeah! That's fine, I'll tell the cook right away." Three minutes later, she has another whole meal on my table ready to eat. It is indeed a cute thing to see. I have this feeling that they were fascinated that a grown man would give up eating meat and cheese and actually admit to being a vegetarian because in this small western town, vegetarians are probably about as common as three-legged hermaphrodites.

Wednesday, September 17, 2003
Day Twenty-One: Arrive Flagstaff, Arizona

Today is my twenty-first day on the road, the longest Kathy and I have been apart in 38 years of marriage. I think I'm getting homesick, I miss Kathy. Right now, if I could just snap my finger and be home, I think I would do it. It crosses my mind that maybe she'll begin to think I don't care about her anymore. At the same time, I also know that she's very independent and would have no problem living by herself if I died. She's not a needy person that seeks attention from me all the time or needs someone to make her feel like she's being taken care of. She was like that even as a young girl, very self-sufficient.

Kathy filled up with tears and sobbed when I pulled out of the driveway leaving on this trip, she's much more emotional than me. She often thinks with her emotions, which can be very endearing. I usually think with my head, I'm more logical. Maybe that's why we're so compatible because we complement one another. Still, on issues like spending money, which can be very emotional, Kathy's extremely careful and disciplined.

I remember in December 1993, when I signed up as one member of a four-man crew to deliver a brand-new 46-foot Beneteau sailboat from Charleston, South Carolina (where it was manufactured) to St. Thomas Island in the Caribbean. I was out to sea for sixteen days with no contact and she was okay with that. She knew it was something I wanted to do at that time and even though it was somewhat dangerous, she never made an issue of the danger. Actually, it did turn out to be dangerous, because we spent slightly more than two full days being banged around by a tropical storm. Anyway, Kathy has always been this way. I think she just accepts the idea that I could be killed or injured pursuing something I love to do. She's not a worry wart in that respect. She wants me to enjoy my life and she accepts the risks that go along with that.

You know, sometimes cheap motel rooms aren't all that bad. I've stayed at expensive motels that have those water savers that take forever to rinse you off. You wind up leaving the shower with soap in your armpits or lodged between your ass cheeks and in back of your balls. I hate those things. This room here in Richfield, Utah is a real dump, but

Wednesday, September 17, 2003
Day Twenty-One: Arrive Flagstaff, Arizona

the bathroom has a great shower head that rinses me down like a fire hose. No soap between my ass cheeks or in back of my balls with this baby!

    I walk over to a restaurant close to my motel and eat a perfect breakfast. Things are still going my way, I hope this keeps up. Next, I really need to re-adjust my seat because I've been sitting on my testicles again. So, I ride across the road to a K-mart and buy a new roll of duct tape. I used up what I brought with me in Bishop, California when I taped over the whole seat to keep out the water. After about thirty minutes of folding the towel, laying it on the seat, testing, folding and testing some more, I think I finally got it right and tape it in place. Once again, I tape over the whole seat because that does keep out the water. Duct tape is amazing!

    Forgetting my eyeglasses were still lying precariously on top of my gas tank, I mount the bike and take off for another day of motorcycle adventures. But, things don't look right, I can't see very well. Oh shit! What happened to my glasses? These are my emergency glasses. I already destroyed my regular glasses by leaving them on top of the bike once, only to have them crushed by an eighteen-wheeler. I quickly pull over next to the entrance of the motel office and start looking at the asphalt pavement with my less than perfect eyesight. Wearing my yellow and black motorcycle jacket and matching full face helmet, I must look like an alien space visitor studying the earth's surface for evidence of tiny life forms.

    Then to my great relief, I spot them, unharmed, lying right beside the bike. They must have fallen off when I parked to look for them. Now I feel good again and I'm off for real this time. Well, not quite, I have to buy gas. Then after that, I realize how cold it is and stop to put on my jacket liner. Will I ever.get started this morning? My new seat design feels good, but once I'm out of town, I realize that pounding wind is still here from yesterday. Fuck! On Route 89 heading south to Arizona, the wind turns indecently cold. I'm dying.

Wednesday, September 17, 2003
Day twenty-One: Arrive Flagstaff, Arizona

It feels like a fridged, 600 mph artic wind is drilling right through my jacket liner. I stop to put on my rain jacket for more protection. That's much better. Now all I have to do is deal with these freakin' wind gusts. I'm being blown all over the road again and I'm holding onto the handlebars with a death grip. No wonder I get tired by five o'clock most days, this is real work.

Finally, I see a sign as I leave the Aspen Prairie, "curves next five miles." Well, this is great, the winds subside because now I'm off the open prairie and into heavily wooded, hilly terrain. I drop down to fourth gear and start playing with the twisty two-lane road. I come upon a string of four cars and effortlessly pass the whole bunch of them, fuck the double lines; those are just for cars and trucks. Hey, I'm having fun now. I approach a semi…can I see far enough ahead to pass? Yeah, it looks clear, but not much time before the next curve. I drop down to third, hit the gas, and I'm around the truck and into the next turn before the trucker even knows what happened. My speed going into the corner is perfect, I give it some gas and scream out of that turn, around another car and into the next turn. This feels good! It sure as hell beats driving a car on the interstate. I pass another string of cars and then the fun's over.

Back to the open Prairie and that slap-happy wind. I'm about eighty miles into my ride for the day when I get to a town called Panguitch. I'm ready for a rest, so I stop for a cup of coffee and an English muffin. Another hundred miles or so and I'm on Alternate 89, which takes me past the north entrance to the Grand Canyon. I've never been to the Northern edge of the Grand Canyon, but the problem is it's 45 miles in and 45 miles back out. I stop for gas and ask an old RV guy if the north edge of the Canyon is any different than the south side because I saw the south side back in the late 1980s. He says, "Yeah it's a lot better, plus, the ride in is better too, very scenic."

Oh, what the hell, I think I'll go for it. With a little luck, I can get in and out and still get to Flagstaff before dark. Parts of the 45-mile ride are beautiful, just like the RV guy told me, with nice curvy roads running through densely wooded forests, then long straight runs through

Wednesday, September 17, 2003
Day twenty-One: Arrive Flagstaff, Arizona

open savannahs with deer and cattle grazing along the side of the road. Great stuff. I get to pass a lot of cars, I love to do that! Passing them on curvy roads is much more fun than the straight roads. The wind in the open areas is brutal though, and slams against the side of the bike like a mean drunk. But soon, I hit more woods again with twisty roads, and the wind dies down. Then surprise, the entrance to the Grand Canyon!

I park the bike and walk to the public overlook for a good view. It's like a short fishing pier that extends out over the edge of the Canyon in back of the main Visitor's Center. It's a great view. Kathy and I visited the southern edge back in the 1980s and when I saw that, I thought it was incredible. Now, I'm looking at the northern edge and the first words that come to mind are, "holy shit." It's the only way I can describe the sight. It's just so immense...and beautiful. The north rim is about 1,500 feet higher than the south rim, but I can't register the difference. Although the southern rim gets more visitors, this side is more natural, remote and more geared for campers and true nature lovers. The southern side is more touristy and commercial.

Standing on the overlook, I glance at the middle-aged woman standing next to me as she takes in the scene. I say, "The only statement I can think of that does this view justice is...holy shit!"

She laughs and says, "I can certainly agree with that."

I look at her again, wondering out loud, "You know those first settlers that came out here in the wagon trains? I wonder what they must have thought when they came upon this unearthly sight."

"They must have fainted," she says, chuckling. I agree and privately think they must have peed their pants wondering, how the hell are we going to get past this!

After taking a bunch of pictures, I get back on my bike to head out. I have to do 45-miles just to get back to break-even on Alternate 89 and get to Flagstaff before dark. On the way out of the visitor's area, several deer are grazing along the road, so I stop and use up the rest of my roll of film on them, then take off again. Back on Alt 89, I gas up at the same station where I gassed up on the way in. Four BMW riders are

Wednesday, September 17, 2003
Day Twenty-One: Arrive Flagstaff, Arizona

just pulling out as I make a call to Kathy on the pay phone. There's no cell phone service out here. She isn't in, so I leave a message that I'll call her later tonight from Flagstaff, then I take off.

I quickly catch up with the BMW riders and pass them. Soon, I'm on the Painted Desert. This is so incredibly beautiful; photos can't possibly capture the beauty of these low mountain plateaus, painted all shades of red and orange. They look like they go on for hundreds of miles and maybe they do. Then there are the vast sand dunes, painted gray, red and black; they look like foothills transplanted here from another planet. All this natural beauty is enhanced even more by the shadows and coloring of the late afternoon sun setting in the distant horizon.

The only bad thing is that the open prairie brings back the wind gusts. The bike is getting slammed back and forth and it takes a lot of energy to stay on the road. I have to squeeze the gas tank between my thighs for leverage so I can fight the wind with my handlebars. I'm able to maintain my speed at 95 mph, but I can tell I'm not going to make Flagstaff before dark. It's just too damn far. I don't like riding at dusk because that's when the deer and other animals come out and it's almost impossible to see them because of all the shadows…I might as well forget it and go on hope and luck. As the sun sets against the far away mountain plateaus, the scene is too gorgeous for my little vocabulary. The horizon glows with color. And finally, as the sun drops behind the long plateaus, they emit an eerie red glow. It's a scene I will not soon forget.

Now, it's dark. The altitude is 8,500 feet. With the wind chill factor, it feels like I'm riding across Antarctica. I can't see worth a shit; I'm flying along at over 90 mph passing caution signs that have pictures of deer with antlers. My helmet and face-shield are coated with bugs. I have to look around and between them. And to make matters more interesting, this strong wind is raising hell with my eyeglass. The frames are crushed against the right side of my face, which makes my glasses

Wednesday, September 17, 2003
Day Twenty-One: Arrive Flagstaff, Arizona

cockeyed, out of focus and smeared with body oil because they are being squished against my skin and eyebrows.

Now my teeth are chattering, and I'm starting to shiver, the first signs of hypothermia. So, I try crouching down behind my low windscreen to reduce the effects of the freezing cold wind, but I can only do this for a few minutes at a time because it's very uncomfortable. I should stop, put on my rain jacket to block the cold wind and clean my glasses, but there isn't any place
to stop and even if there were, I wouldn't be able to see it because I'm going too fast. There's a fair amount of traffic, and it's totally dark in the desert. They really should put street lights out here...just for me.

About the time I'm ready to give up, I spot a sign that reads, *Flagstaff City Limits*. Hurray, I made it! Then, about ten minutes later and not a moment too soon, I see a Super 8 Motel. They have a room. Thank God! That's it for today. I find a bar and grill close by. They have Heineken, but nothing for me to eat. The bartender says, with a smart-ass attitude, "We're not a vegetarian-friendly place."

The next place I try is Mexican. They have plenty of food for me to eat but no beer. Well, you gotta take the good with the bad, I think to myself.

Thursday, September 18, 2003
Day Twenty-Two: Arrive Lordsburg, New Mexico

I'm far from a religious person, but I had a dream last night about talking to God. The idea is that God is in every human. Our souls or spirits are part of the God consciousness. In the dream, I was told that everything is a manifestation of God consciousness, including, of course, we humans. The dream reminds me of a quote by Max Planck, the Nobel Prize-winning physicist that is considered the father of quantum mechanics. He famously said, "All matter originates and exists only by virtue of a force...we must assume behind this force the existence of a conscious and intelligent mind. This mind is the matrix of all matter." Planck felt that consciousness is primary to matter and all matter emerges from this single consciousness.

    I have to get on the road. However, before I do that, I have to adjust my chain again. I'm getting quite good at this. After that, I think I'll head south to I-10 and follow that home. It goes through South Texas and I can deviate from I-10 and take an excursion farther south if I want to. But basically, what I really want to do is go home.

    This morning, I discovered my rain jacket was coming apart at the seams from too much flapping in the wind. It's a good thing I'm heading closer to home, things are starting to fall apart. I'm afraid the bike will be next. I take I-17 South from Flagstaff to Phoenix. As soon as I get on the road, it registers with me how much I like my motorcycle. I'm thinking to myself, I like being on top of this bike, feeling the way it handles, moving around other vehicles, the virtually instant power response when I turn the throttle. It's a great experience, the whole thing.

    I'm cruising along now on I-17 in the low 90s and I'm pulling up beside this gray Toyota sedan. I'm in the right (slow) lane. The Toyota is in the fast lane to my left. I'm a few feet behind him when I figure I'll just pass him, but as I get closer, he goes faster. I'm looking at my speedometer, 95, then 97, 98, 99, 100 mph. I decide to keep up with him and see what happens. Now we're doing 105 mph and he's still a foot or two in front of me in the left lane. This is a young male driver. I figure he wants to see how fast he has to go before I give up. There aren't any

Thursday, September 18, 2003
Day Twenty-Two: Arrive Lordsburg, New Mexico

cars in front of us, so I decide to pass him and see how he reacts. I drop down into fifth gear and run ahead until he's just a tiny spot in my rearview mirror. I'm doing 135 mph and I slow back down to about 100 and see him in my mirror slowly catching up to me. He must have it floored.

When he pulls up beside me, we do the same thing all over again. Only this time, I don't wait for him to catch up. That was fun, I feel like a kid. About 45 miles north of Phoenix, I see a sign, "Elevation 2000-feet," and within a couple of minutes, it starts to get warm. A few minutes after that, it feels like an oven. In another few minutes, I enter city traffic and everything gets bogged down: terrible traffic, congestion, brutal heat, tractor-trailer trucks, delivery trucks, cars, RVs and more heat. The morning started out really well, great breakfast, fun ride in beautiful weather, now it's hot as hell and I'm in the middle of slow city traffic. It has to be at least 105 degrees. I'm thinking of stopping to consider an alternate route, but I can't stop, too much traffic and I don't know the area. Then I reason, maybe it's better to stay on the interstate, I may just get out of the city and into cooler weather faster.

After passing through city-center on I-17, I see a sign for I-10 to Tucson. That's my turn off. Maybe I-10 will bring me into some better weather. After I get back out in the open country, it's still hot, but not like the oven intensity of downtown Phoenix. The Interstate is so boring. I'm cruising along at between 90 and 100 mph and notice some kid in a red Honda Accord is pacing me just to my rear. Another game. I speed up, he speeds up. I move quickly and pass some cars and he follows. Then, when there's a long open space with no traffic, I leave him in the dust, then slow down a little so he can catch me. He floors his Honda and I watch him in my rearview mirror as he slowly catches up. Then we do the same thing all over again. I think he is just as bored as I am. It gives us something to do

I have to stand up on my foot pegs every few minutes to let some fresh air blow through my crotch. The only good thing about the interstate is that it's fast. But the scenery sucks, it's just a lot of prairie

Thursday, September 18, 2003
Day Twenty-Two: Arrive Lordsburg, New Mexico

with low mountains in the background. The landscape is full of Saguaro Cacti. These are tall cacti that look like stick figures of a human with two or three arms standing on one leg

I see I'm coming up on two guys on Harleys loaded down with traveling gear. They're moving along at about 70 mph. I whiz past them doing about 100 and give a little wave as I go by. They probably think I'm just another dickhead on a Jap bike. This riding is uneventful, just lots of flat prairie broken up with some small towns. I spot an exit that looks like a decent sized town, because it has a Holiday Inn, and I leave I-10. I've been on the road for eight hours and a warm shower, a cold beer and some food seems very appealing right now.

The town I stop in is called Lordsburg, New Mexico, about 150-miles east of El Paso on I-10. I check into the first motel I see with a sign for rooms under 30-dollars, a "Motel 10." It's a dive, of course, but I get to park right at my front door, so it's easy to unload my bike and that's worth a lot. Also, after I check-in, I find out the shower is first class, the room is Spartan but big. After I clean up, I get back on the bike and look for a brew and some dinner. I get lost and ask some guy working on his truck in front of his house to direct me to a bar. He gives me some complicated directions in broken English that I couldn't possibly follow without a programmable GPS and a language translator. So, I go back to the motel and start over again.

This time I find a restaurant but the hostess says, "No beer." She does give me directions to another place, however. I go that way, which takes me to the actual downtown area. It's dead…vacant buildings, dismal looking old shops and lots of gravel on the road. I finally hit the center of town. I know it's the center because that's where the stoplight is, the only one in town, just as the hostess told in her directions. It's really just a blinking light at this time of day, 7PM. Most of the people here seem to be American Indian or Mexican. It's dusk and the town looks like an old movie scene from the depression era with sagebrush blowing across barren streets, railroad tracks with idle, empty boxcars

Thursday, September 18, 2003
Day Twenty-Two: Arrive Lordsburg, New Mexico

and far too many vacant buildings. Coming from busy South Florida, it's hard to believe towns like this still exist in America.

I find the bar, park, walk in and look around. It's dark and I see about five crusty working-guys sitting at the bar nursing Buds. The bartender/owner says he's closing at 7:30 because he's tired and wants to go home, "I've had enough of these customers for one day," he tells me and gives me directions to a good Mexican restaurant with a bar down the street and across the railroad tracks.

I find this place, walk in and it's packed full of people. The only remaining seat is at the bar, which is my preference anyway. The guy to my left is wearing a black leather vest and a big black cowboy hat. He has dozens of little medallions and insignias pinned to his vest. I sit down next to him, order a Heineken, look over, make eye contact and say, "Hi," to which he replies in kind. I ask him, "Are you a tourist or do you live here?"

"I'm a tourist," he says. "I'm just riding through town."

"On a motorcycle?" I ask.

"Yeah, sure am."

"So am I," I say.

Well, that conversation leads to two-hours of bull-shiting about motorcycles and motorcycle travel. It turns out he rides a 1999 black Goldwing and lives in Sunnyville, Arizona, near Phoenix. It's a

retirement village. He's taking a tour by himself of the areas within a few hundred miles around Phoenix. Not a high mileage ride, just a reason to get out on his bike and go someplace
for a week or so

When I describe my bike to him, he's curious why an old guy like me would ride a fast, uncomfortable bike like mine. "I like the incredible acceleration and handling," I tell him. He still doesn't get it, but we have fun talking anyway.

We order dinner there at the bar while we discuss the broader philosophical aspects of motorcycling if there actually is such a thing. And then we swap stories about our motorcycle adventures from the

Thursday, September 18, 2003
Day Twenty-Two: Arrive Lordsburg, New Mexico

past. He tells me about his big bike trip up to Alaska, where he actually lived for a while. I'm fascinated by the story and ask a lot of questions because that's something I dream of doing someday. Maybe, on that new Yamaha FJR 1300. The guy's leather vest is something else, the front is covered with gold medallions, at least 20 on each side. He says most of them are from his ride to Alaska. He's also wearing a big black cowboy hat and he has one of those beards without the mustache, you know, like one of those old-fashioned Mormon guys.

He's been married for 18 years to a woman that is really into RV motorhomes. He tells me, "She has a 31-footer right now and she belongs to a woman's RV association." He says he reluctantly goes on motorhome trips with her but really prefers his Goldwing.

He likes to ride alone, he tells me, and like me, doesn't much care for biker groups or crowds. I am a bit shocked when he uses the word "nigger" in a joke. I just give him a stone-faced look and I can tell from the pregnant pause he gets the message.

When I get my check, I'm surprised to see the Heineken only cost me two-dollars each, a lot less than the $4.50 to $5.50 I pay at home. In fact, I ate two burrito dinners and drank three beers and the whole check still only came to 13-bucks. Unbelievable. That's almost enough incentive to move here.

When we are ready to leave, he says, "I've got to see this Honda Blackbird of yours, I've never ridden a bike like that." We walk outside together and he gives the bike a close inspection, asks a lot of questions about the horsepower, type of engine, the low handlebars, etc.

"How fast does this thing go?" he asks.

"Well, I've had it up to the low 170s more times than I can count, but I only did one actual top-speed run and that was 188 mph on the speedometer. It gets up to 170 real fast, after that, acceleration slows a bit and after 180, it slows a lot. So you need a long, clear road with no intersections or access roads. He shook his head indicating that was not for him and maybe I was a bit loony.

Friday, September 19, 2003
Day Twenty-Three: Arrive Marfa, Texas

I'm thinking about the Goldwing guy I met last night. He talked a lot about the wind gusts riding through the prairie and desert areas during certain times of the year. He said these gusts commonly reach 45-50 mph and they knock motorcycles all over the road. Some people, he said, won't ride in them…too dangerous. Plus, he said, it's incredibly stressful. It takes a lot of effort just to hang on to the handlebars and stay in your own lane.

He was the one that brought up the subject of wind gusts and then really went on about it. I couldn't help smiling because I thought, that's precisely the way I feel. I wondered if maybe I was over-reacting or perhaps it was my imagination, or maybe I was just a pussy about the whole thing. But I feel better after hearing that he feels the same way.

I eat breakfast at the beer-less diner I tried to eat at last night where the hostess directed me across town. It was an excellent breakfast. At this point, I decide I want to head straight home on I-10. I've seen about all I want to see and I miss Kathy. And yes, I miss my greyhound, Eddy, too. I figure I should be home sometime on Monday. I'm only going to ride about seven hours a day, no marathon rides like in '97.

It's tough for me to get on the road early. It's already 10 o'clock and I'm still farting around. But there's no rush. It's a little cool, so I put on my jacket liner and neck-scarf. Once I'm on the road, I feel good. But, that annoying and persistent wind is still here. It's coming from about 2 o'clock and it's steady, no gusts. My bike has a constant lean of about ten degrees as I cruise along at 90 mph. My helmet is pressed hard against my right cheek, causing my eyeglasses to be constantly cockeyed and out of focus. I don't remember all this wind on my 1997 trip. But, that trip was in July. Maybe, that's the difference. I see vast expanses of flat prairie land, lots of fifth wheelers and motor homes, all going somewhere, exploring the great American west. Lucky people, us travelers; millions of people will never be this fortunate.

A pickup passes me in the opposite direction towing a very well preserved 1947 Cadillac. I know it's a '47 model because in 1954 when I was a young boy of 12 in South Florida, the couple down the block used to own one. The wife was beautiful, at least to a 12-year old boy. But,

Friday, September 19, 2003
Day Twenty-Three: Arrive Marfa, Texas

the thing that makes me remember her is that she always wore a top that showed a lot of her breasts. Sometimes she would bend over while we talked and I could see everything. Quite a thrill for a boy my young age. But, the thing I recall best is that she had a lot of hair on her chest, just like a man. I'll never forget that woman or her black '47 Caddy that was parked in front of their house.

Now I see this one being towed with the front wheels up on a little trailer. The guy probably just bought it from someone that's had it in their garage for the last fifty years and now he's taking it home, maybe because his father owned one.

The trains out west are a lot longer than the east. I'm looking at one now and it appears to be a good mile long, hauling cattle, new cars, oil, containers, you name it. They go slow but they don't stop much, kind of like an ocean freighter on land. The Interstate also has a steady caravan of 18-wheelers traveling across the southern US, five and six in a line. They remind me of those big military convoys during war operations. I just weave through them as I move along. That's the nice part about motorcycles, there is always room to pass.

As I'm cruising along, contemplating all this in my mind, a young guy in a black Ultima GXE slowly passes me on my left. No trucks close by right now. He's doing about 95 and I'm doing about 90. I decide to increase my speed just enough to keep up with him. Now he speeds up to 100 mph. I pace him. Now my front wheel is right beside his right rear tire. He speeds up some more, 101, 102, 105.

Now he's up to 108 mph and he levels off at that speed, so I pull up next to his passenger door and pace him for a little, while I wait to see what he wants to do next.

I'm coming up on the back of a semi in my lane, so I drop down to fifth gear and quickly move in front of the Ultima. I pass the semi and just keep the gas on until the Ultima is just a dot in my mirror. I get up to 130 mph and slow back down again to about 100. The road is clear and I see the Ultima pulling up on me again, he's trying hard to catch me, so I know he wants to play. Unfortunately, we both run into another long

Friday, September 19, 2003
Day Twenty-Three: Arrive Marfa, Texas

caravan of trucks blocking both lanes. I slow down a little and drop behind the Ultima. Now we're both in the left lane, waiting for an opening. Finally, a window opens in the right lane to get around the Semi directly in front of us, but the opening won't last long.

The Ultima's right blinker flashes, he moves to the right like he's going for it and pulls back, not enough room. But, I can see there is still enough room for me if I'm quick. I flash my right turn signal, drop down to fourth, move into the left lane and shoot around the semi, just as the opening closes. Now I've got open road as far as I can see in the left lane, so I run up to 140 or so for a while, and gradually settle back to about 105 as I move over to the right lane. Now I wait to see how long it takes for the Ultima to catch me. It takes a while, but I see him getting bigger and bigger in my rear-view mirror.

Finally, he catches me in the left lane and we pace each other for a few moments. What do we do now? I look over at him and give him a friendly little wave, which he returns. Then, I take off again at a speed I know he can't possibly match. Hey, that was fun. You need something to break up the monotony of the interstate.

I-10 has a lot of signs that say, "Dust Storms may exist next 15 miles." Sometimes it's ten miles. I also see signs saying, "Zero visibility possible." Usually, I see these signs shortly after the "Dust storm" signs. All this wind is pretty common out here.

I was thinking today about the Goldwing rider at the bar last night. He said, "I don't know if I could ever feel comfortable or safe enough to take a motorcycle up to 140 or 150 mph, it just seems too dangerous."

I said, "Hell, the tires are rated at over 200 mph, if the bolts are tight, you just have to have a little faith. Plus, if you do it a few times you get used to it."

"I guess you're right," he said, "but I don't think that's for me."

I find myself drifting off in thought a lot on the interstate, daydreaming. That's why I want to leave as much space between me and

Friday, September 19, 2003
Day Twenty-Three: Arrive Marfa, Texas

other cars as possible. On the other hand, I usually go faster than the regular flow of traffic to keep things interesting and so I don't have to be concerned about drivers pulling up in back of me. I'm mainly concerned with the ones in front.

I always see flies around the front of my bike when I stop for gas. After thinking about this, I realize I haven't washed any bugs off the bike since I left home. The bike probably smells a lot like dead meat to the flies; like 'hey guys, dinner just pulled in, let's go!'

Now I'm about 120 miles east of El Paso and I'm running short on gas, so I'm pulling off at a town called Vanhorn. My ass is sore and my legs ache in the area behind my knees. I don't know what that means, but I'm pretty sure it has something to do with getting old. I keep straightening my legs out while I'm riding, but it doesn't do much good. The only thing that really helps is getting off the bike and walking around a bit.

I fill up with gas and buy a small bottle of water at the convenience store. While I'm killing time walking around, I see this big wall map of Texas. It shows right where I am, here in Vanhorn. Next, I see where Route 90 departs from I-10, right here in Vanhorn, and heads farther south then goes east to San Antonio, which is where I'm headed anyway. I hate riding on I-10, and I would love to get back on a secondary road that will take me through some interesting country. I ask a few people hanging around how far it is to the next town with a motel and restaurants on Route 90. They say about 70 to 75 miles. Well, that's about one hour away at the max. It's 6 o'clock now. I figure I'll be okay if I can find a motel by 7PM.

That sounds good and I take off south on Route 90 to see what happens. Right away, I feel better. I pass a car going in the opposite direction every two or three miles, lots of cattle, horses and small, abandoned towns. I pass one vacant town and spot a washed-out storefront with "El Cheapo General Store" still visible across the front. These places have been out of business for many years and more likely,

Friday, September 19, 2003
Day Twenty-Three: Arrive Marfa, Texas

many decades. Probably victims of Interstate 10. I stop and take a few pictures because it's all so original and real, this is not Disney World.

Finally, I get to a town called Marfa…population 1200, seventy-four miles from Vanhorn. Riding into town, it looks like the place has been abandoned. Then, I see a gas station that's open for business. A little farther along, I see a motel; but from the appearance, it's been closed for years. A bit farther I see more signs of life, but no motels. I head back to where I came into town and I see a motel that I missed on the way in called The Holiday Capri Inn. VACANCY. Just what I'm looking for at $37 per night with no discounts for AARP. The owner tells me this is one of only two motels in town. The other one is on the other side of town and there's a hotel in the center of town.

I don't argue; I feel lucky to find a room. After I put away my stuff, I ask the owner where I can find a bar to get a beer and maybe some dinner. "The only place to get both is the Hotel in the center of town," she tells me with a deadpan expression. "Just ride to the blinking stop light in the center of town and make a left, go down two blocks, you can't miss it." I follow her directions but I can't really see it. I circle around the block and then, oh yeah, I see it now, the "El Paisano Hotel." The plaque near the front entrance says, "This Property has been placed on, The NATIONAL REGISTER of HISTORIC PLACES." I park my bike, walk in and surprise! This is a high-class place. Everything shouts, "quality." What's a place like this doing here in this god-forsaken town? It seems entirely out of place.

I ask at the front desk, "How much does it cost to stay here for one night?"

She answers, "Rooms run between $90 and $170, but we don't have any vacancies." I look around and the place is almost deserted, no business, no people milling around…where are they? Is this a ghost hotel? I see an open patio dining area with a few people eating dinner, but it's 7:30 on a Friday night, the place should be packed with diners. I ask the desk clerk, "Where's the bar?" And she points across the patio.

Friday, September 19, 2003
Day Twenty-Three: Arrive Marfa, Texas

So, I walk across the courtyard and through the double French doors leading to a spacious room with a big circular bar. No customers This is very strange. The young lady behind the bar is strikingly attractive and looks about 28, blond hair, trim body with a great smile.

I sit down and she asks, "What would you like?"

"Do you have Heineken?"

"Yes, sure," she says and brings one over as I lay my helmet and jacket on the chair next to me. Now, I'm the only customer at the bar and all this young bartender has to do is take care of me, so naturally, we start talking. She asks what I'm doing in town.

"I'm just passing through" I answer. "I'm on a motorcycle vacation." Then I add, "That's my motorcycle across the street." She can see it out the window.

"Where are all the people?" I ask. "The desk clerk said the place is full

"Oh, that's because every Friday night all the Hotel guests are invited to a big Bar-B-Q at a local ranch not far from here, it's an old tradition at the hotel. So yeah, the place does look kind of empty right now."

Her name is Samantha, not Sam or Sammi but Samantha. Samantha tells me she grew up in Laredo, Texas which is about 150 miles south of San Antonio, right along the Mexican border. Right now, she lives here in Marfa with her parents. "I'm designing a line of women's casual wear. My dad is going to help me with the manufacturing of the garments, close by in Mexico." As our conversation moves along, she tells me she has also lived in Australia, Sri Lanka, off the coast of India and a few other places. Maybe she's trying to impress me, I think to myself. She also volunteers that she's 31, has a boyfriend but has never been married.

Then she tells me a little about her equally attractive co-worker and friend, Stephanie, the waitress that handles the indoor and patio tables who just joined us. "Stephanie," she says, looking at Stephanie

Friday, September 19, 2003
Day Twenty-Three: Arrive Marfa, Texas

with a mischievous smile, "graduated from acting school in New York City and has never had an acting job but, she did appear on the David Letterman show once." She then asks Stephanie to tell me the story.

So Stephanie, cheekily proud of her so far misguided education, laughs and sits down next to me. "So what happened?" I innocently ask.

"Well, I always wanted to be an actress and my parents put me through acting school in New York City, then, the one and only time they ever saw me on TV I was drunk."

"Really? Your mom and dad must have been tickled pink," I chuckled.

"Oh yeah," she smiled. "I was featured on David Letterman once. The segment was, People That Drink Before Noon. Then she goes on to tell me, "My friends and I had a day off from school and we were hanging out at our favorite pub one morning having a few beers. Suddenly, the Letterman crew walks in and David conducts an entire segment of his show right from our table, talking mostly to me. He was teasing us about drinking before noon. He checked out our drinks to see what kind of booze we were drinking and generally having a lot of fun with us. My mother, a very proper lady, saw it and she almost died. So," she grins, "that's my only public exposure as a result of acting school."

Now, both girls are hanging with me at the bar. Stephanie is sitting next to me and Samantha is on the other side of the bar. Very relaxed with her elbows on the bar and her chin in her palms, looking at me. I feel like I'm the only person on her mind. She tells me more about her life in Texas and expresses curiosity about my aimless motorcycle trip and how I had accidentally found this little town.

"Do you know that this town is where *Giant* was filmed, starring James Dean, Elizabeth Taylor and Rock Hudson?" Elisabeth asks. I admit that I saw the movie many years ago, but have no clue about how or where it was filmed.

"Well, let me tell you," she smiles. "This hotel was where all the actors stayed while filming the movie."

Friday, September 19, 2003
Day Twenty-Three: Arrive Marfa, Texas

"So," I reply, "that's what all the famous actor's pictures in the men's room are about, and the ones in the main lobby."

"You got it! This is a very famous hotel. People come from all over to stay here," she says with a bit of pride.

I ask her about the old movie theater I saw down the street called *The Palace Theater*. "Oh, that's closed up, but," she adds, "that's where the movie, *Giant,* was premiered, or at least, that's one of the theaters."

It turns out this town does have a fascinating history, even aside from the historical movie.

Samantha goes on to tells me, "Donald Judd, a famous painter, lived here and worked here for a long time before he died. Also, Tommy Lee Jones, the actor, among other notable people, loves to come here and stay in this hotel to get away and find a little peace and quiet."

Now I'm getting hungry, so I ask Samantha for a menu. Surprise, surprise. The menu lists a vegan salad. "Way out here in the middle of cow country, a menu with the word vegan. What is this world coming to?" I jokingly ask Samantha.

"Like I told you, people come here from all over the place, so we cater to all tastes." She's equally surprised that an old motorcycle guy like me would be a vegan, which leads to another whole conversation. I order the salad, a side of their specially seasoned and roasted red potatoes, along with some steamed and seasoned broccoli. It is all very first class in taste and presentation. The most enjoyable meal I've had on this trip.

I know the place is old when I go to the men's room; they have separate faucets for the hot and cold water...very old-school stuff like you see in parts of Europe, but rarely in the US. I drink more than my share of Heineken and enjoy chatting with the two young beauties. We talk at length about motorcycles, acting, and Samanthas endeavor at manufacturing the clothes she designed. She's negotiating for employees and factory space in Mexico right now, with the help of her father and the Mayor of a small Mexican border town just south of Laredo. Stephanie keeps trying to tell me funny stories about her nowhere acting

Friday, September 19, 2003
Day Twenty-Three: Arrive Marfa, Texas

career between occasional interruptions from her two customers on the patio. A very entertaining girl, this Stephanie.

I feel very awkward because both of these young women seem genuinely interested in me. Samantha looks directly at me as we talk. She isn't just talking about herself either, she's pumping me for more information about my adventures and my life in general. I'm really not used to this kind of interest from beautiful young females. I can't help but wonder if she is just milking me for a big tip? After all, except for three or four guys that popped in and out of the bar for drinks, I'm her best customer for the night. Nah, I think I'll believe she just thought I was a cool older guy, that feels a lot better.

The evening has been so outstanding, I think it's best to quit while I'm ahead. So, with some regrets, I pay my bill, leave a very generous tip, and go back to my motel for a good night sleep. As I ride back to my motel, I'm thinking about my rear tire. Why am I not thinking about Samantha and Stephanie? Age, I guess. That and the fact that I have my own beautiful woman waiting for me at home. The wear lines, those little raised areas between the tire treads that tell you it's time to replace the tire, are starting to show. The problem isn't that the tire will just explode while I'm riding down the highway at 90 mph, it's just that it's a lot easier to get a flat tire because the rubber offers less protection against glass or nails; it's thinner. Almost every motorcycle or car flat I've ever had was on a worn tire.

I'm also concerned about my chain because the chain adjustment gauge indicates "replace chain." I've never had one break on me, but usually strange noises start emanating from the bike as a warning. I'm not there yet, but I'm not far away either. The only reason I'm thinking about this now is that Samantha and the Motel owner both highly recommended I visit Big Bend National Park, which is about 150 miles out of my way and there are no bike repair shops down in that area.

I also remember Kathy telling me her research indicated Big Bend was a great place to visit as well. My brother, Bob, and his wife, Pat, highly recommended it too. In fact, Bob and Pat said Big Bend was

Friday, September 19, 2003
Day Twenty-Three: Arrive Marfa, Texas

the most beautiful National Park they ever visited and they have seen them all...literally. How could I not go with these kinds of recommendations? I can't pass it up. I'll just hope the bike stays together until I get to another big town.

Speaking of bike maintenance, I'm also about 800-miles overdue for an oil change. Oh, the problems of being a traveler. Life is just full of little risks and difficulties. I'll take this chance though because I don't know how long it will be before I ever get back to this part of the country.

Saturday, September 20, 2003
Day Twenty-Four: Arrive Del Rio, Texas

Last night, I had a dream that I was visiting a university here in the west. I was invited by a few of the students to a big outdoor music festival. The festival looked pretty normal except most of the kids were on blankets, dressed up like American Indians, lots of pretty feathers, deer skins with white and fawn trimming and colored beads.

In the dream, it dawned on me that I had to pee. On my way to a more private area, I was walking between the students, trying not to step on their blankets. When I looked closer, I saw a lot of the students were down on the ground making out with one another. Then, I noticed they weren't just making out. Inside all those feathers and beads, they were going down on each other and fucking each other. Lots of girls were eating each other's pussies and in some cases, a girl and a boy were both working between a girl's legs

The students who weren't having sex were ignoring the ones right next to them who were going at it. Instead, they were watching the concert up front. I couldn't believe this was really happening. I sauntered down the narrow path that split the students into two separate groups, as I made my way to the men's room. I couldn't help getting a stiff erection. All I was wearing was an Indian robe, it was open in the front and I was having a hard time concealing my state of arousal. That's all I remember; too bad, it was nice while it lasted. I guess my dream was a residual effect of my encounter last night with Samantha and Stephanie. As I'm getting out of bed, I look around the room and realize, this is no more than a $25 place, max. The one unique feature about this room: a fly swatter. How sweet, just like a Marriott.

I eat breakfast at a tiny Mexican café on Main Street. Mostly cowboy types eat here. There are cowboy hats, jeans, and lots of "Howdy Boys" when a couple of new cowboys walk in together, kind of the standard greeting between these guys.

After breakfast, I head for Big Bend National Forrest by way of Route 67 South. About 50 miles south, southwest of Marfa, I hit Presidio, Texas. Now, this is an interesting town. It's right along the Rio Grande River, with a population of about five thousand. The actual settlement goes back to 1,500 CE when farmers first started to grow

Saturday, September 20, 2003
Day Twenty-Four: Arrive Del Rio, Texas

stuff here on a regular basis. And I'll tell you, some of the buildings look just about that old.

In the center of town, there's a stop light, a convenience store and a cow. You got it right, there's a lone cow, lazily grazing on the grass in front of the convenience store. This is a very laid-back place. I also can't help but notice, there's no organization or structure to the layout of the community. Talk about a need for zoning laws. You have a broken down mobile home and a house on the same lot in the center of town, a typical arrangement around the West, but not downtown. On the edge of town is a beautiful house on a hill. It looks like a million bucks just sitting there. But all around the house are old, dilapidated cars and other junk, like refrigerators and old lawn equipment. This would not fly in my town, Cooper City, Florida, where homeowners get a citation for too much mold on their tile roofs.

After leaving Presidio, I get onto Route 170 West and head for Big Bend. What a beautiful ride. The weather is perfect and the scenery is gorgeous with lots of twisty, curvy roads and hills. And I do mean a lot of hills: big hills, small hills and everything in between. It's like a fun roller coaster ride from my childhood. There are even signs posted to warn motorists about the 15% plus grades. It's like this…go over the top of a hill, gas it on the way down, hit the low point, then fly up the next hill while your stomach lags a moment or two behind the whole process. I couldn't help myself from yelling out like a big kid on a roller coaster ride. This is fun stuff!

The Big Bend area has had a lot of rain lately, so the whole place is verdant and alive. The scene reminds me of the Spielberg movie, "Jurassic Park." I ride out to a viewing point called Chisos Basin. The turns are so sharp that I almost have to get off the bike and walk it around the corner. These are very sharp switchback turns with unbelievable inclines as you near the top of the mountain. The ride is well worth it though. I can't help but shout, "WOW! This is so fucking beautiful." The place has bears, deer, mountain lions, pretty much the

Saturday, September 20, 200
Day Twenty-Four: Arrive Del Rio, Texas

whole outdoors thing. I get some excellent pictures of a mother deer and her two babies munching on the tall grass.

On the way back to Route 170, I see signs warning about loose livestock. I'm still gassing it on the way down the hills to get the roller coaster effect until I get to the crest of the next hill, and then I slow down to approximately the actual speed limit. In this case, it's 40 mph. Just as I'm cresting this one hill, a little black and white pig scoots across the road, not more than one second in front of my path. Damn, that was close, I'm glad I slowed down. If I had been going a little bit faster, that could have been the end of my trip…and the little pig.

Not two minutes later, something else happens. I come upon a long copper-colored snake busy trying to slither across the road. I don't want to run him over, so I swerve the bike. I believe I just missed him. At worst, I may have clipped his tail. He covered my whole lane of the road. I had to cross the centerline to get around him. You don't see these kinds of snakes where I live, maybe 50 years ago but not anymore, too many people. Big Bend is indeed a remarkable and beautiful place, but it's getting late and I need to get back closer to civilization. So, I head for Route 395 which leads me back to Route 90, a 70-mile ride and a lovely ride too.

Back on Route 90, I head east to the next town, Marathon. I figure I'll stop there for the night because the town after that is another 123 miles. I arrive in Marathon at 3:30, right on schedule. The only problem is…there's no restaurant. Now I have to go to plan B and ride to Del Rio, 123 miles farther east.

I'm getting cold. So, I stop to put on my jacket liner. The next thing I know, it's raining, very light, but rain nonetheless. I can handle this without rain gear, as long as it doesn't start pouring. Only seventy-five more miles to go. The rain is getting heavier. Pretty soon, I'm tucked behind my windscreen to keep the rain off me. I'm not stopping to put on that damn rain gear. I've got well over nine hours in the saddle After riding in the rain for another hour, I'm tired, worried about my

Saturday, September 20, 200
Day Twenty-Four: Arrive Del Rio, Texas

loose chain, wet, cold and hungry. Just about the time I'm ready to file a lawsuit against Mother Nature and borrow a gun to shoot my motorcycle, I ride into Del Rio and spot a Motel Six! I pay the $37 and check-in. Next, I have to eat. So, I ride over to the Chili's restaurant I saw on the way into town.

    Even though it's early, it's Saturday night and the place is packed and loud. I find an empty stool at the bar and order a beer. My body is damp and it feels cold. There are about six guys on the other side of the bar drinking Buds from a bucket. The whole bunch of them are yelling and hollering like they're at a football game. They look like they just got off work with their paychecks. They can't leave too soon for me. Then Magically, the waitress gives them their checks. Five minutes later, the place is quiet…maybe things are starting to go my way again. I relax, drink a beer and order a bean burger with a side of steamed veggies. Man, that tastes good, so I order the same thing all over again. At 8:30. I call Kathy. No Answer. It's only 9:30 her time. She probably went out for dinner. I'm ready for bed.

Sunday, September 21, 2003
Day Twenty-Five: Arrive San Antonio, Texas

I spend 45-minutes talking to Kathy and tease her about being out so late. She says, "it was Saturday night and I needed to get out of the house, so Eddy and I went to downtown Hollywood. We split a pizza outside Mama Mia's and then walked over to the Octopus for a drink. I got to talking to an interesting couple, a man and a woman. Time flew by and we got home a little late," she says sweetly.

"Yeah, sure, likely story," I say smiling, trying to give her a hard time ."

"No, really," she says, like maybe I doubted her. "I told them all about you and your motorcycling trip. We're supposed to see them again next Saturday, same place after you get back." I feel renewed after our long conversation.

I get my shit together and head for my bike, which is parked right outside my door. As I'm walking out the front door, I see this guy that owns the Kawasaki 650 off-road I saw last night when I pulled in; it's parked next to my Blackbird. The guy is dressed just like me: jeans, black t-shirt and black boots. I say, "Are you doing some off-road riding around this area?"

"No," he answers, I'm just traveling the western states."

"By yourself?" I ask.

"Yeah, sure!" He answers me like, 'Doesn't everybody?'

"Me too," I reply, thinking this is strange, why is he riding this dorky off-road bike if he is traveling around the country? I know some guys prefer all-terrain bikes. BMW makes a popular one...and very expensive too. So, I ask, "You're touring around the west on this?"

"Yeah, it's a great touring bike." He answers like he's surprised I didn't already know this.

"So, how fast can you cruise on a bike like this, 75-80 mph?" I ask.

"Oh, faster than that," he says. "I can cruise 95 easy, even faster, like 105 or 110 if I want to, but 95 is easy."

He's bullshitting me a little bit because the top speed this bikes is only about 105-110 but you can't cruise at that speed. I let it go. His bike is taller than mine and higher off the ground. It's also, narrow and light,

Sunday, September 21, 2003
Day Twenty-Five: Arrive San Antonio, Texas

with a modest two-cylinder motor. Not exactly a powerhouse, but they are comfortable to ride and very capable of long-distance road trips. The guy looks about five-feet-eight with a modest pot belly that droops over his belt just a bit. I'd guess he's about 48 to 50 in age.

He's a friendly sort and tells me his name is Don. He has a scraggly, short, salt and pepper beard and a mostly bald head, like mine. Don tells me he's an aerospace engineer from San Diego, California and that every chance he gets to travel, his motorcycle is what he travels on, if possible. His trips are usually in line with his job. Sometimes he'll get an assignment to work a few days, say, in Houston. And he'll ride his bike instead of going by car or plane. "I still get the same reimbursement rate from my company," he tells me, clearly happy with the arrangement.

Then he tells me he's also a professional photographer. He shows me a seven-inch by ten-inch electronic tablet and says, "Watch this." Then he pushes a button and photos of beautiful women in various stages of dress appear in a series of about one second apart. The pictures are all magazine quality and some are very sexy, if not blatantly erotic, the kind of stuff you'd see in Penthouse or Playboy. I'm beginning to think this is one lucky guy. He has not one, but two great hobbies, motorcycling and photographing beautiful, sexy women.

He tells me he's publishing a book of these very pictures, "The book should be out pretty soon," he says. Then I've also done some magazine pictorials for nightclubs."

"You mean, like strip joints?" I ask.

"Yeah, that kind of stuff," he says. "I go around to the different clubs, take action shots of the girls in their acts and then I do a little write-up for the club to put in the magazine along with the pictures." I've seen these magazines; most strip joints distribute them for free in the entrance lobby. They're a glossy magazine of extremely sexy advertisements for the entire sex industry in a particular area: escort services, massage parlors, swinger clubs and of course, strip clubs.

Sunday, September 21, 2003
Day Twenty-Five: Arrive San Antonio, Texas

He tells me he's ridden all over the country on his Kawasaki off-road. He's got a girlfriend in North Dakota that he rides up to visit, which led to him telling me a couple of stories about riding in snow and 30-degree weather. "It sucks big time," he says. But the one thing that scares him the most is lightening. "I had a photo shoot scheduled a couple of days from now in Houston with this exquisitely beautiful and slender, black girl. I called and canceled because of the thunderstorms east of here."

"Shit, that's where I'm headed this morning, east!" I grimace. I have to go through San Antonio to get some work done on my bike. Plus, that's the route I take to get home."

"Not me," he says. "I'm heading north to avoid the thunderstorms. There's a lot of open prairie east of here, I don't want to get caught out there with lightning all around me."

I ask him if he likes to ride alone. He says, "I don't really like to ride with other motorcyclists, I've had lots of offers, but you have to make too many compromises. They want to go too slow; they want to stop too often, or not often enough, etc., etc."

"That's exactly how I feel. You summed it up perfectly," I chuckle. He's about ready to take off by now, so we bid each other farewell and I add, "Stay safe!"

"Fuck that...don't you stay safe; it's boring."

Then I say, "Okay, have fun instead."

"Okay," he hollers as he pulls out, then he gives me a friendly wave goodbye.

'An odd duck,' I think as I watched him leave. That's what I called him during our long conversation. When I said that, he smiled. I could tell he took it as a compliment. Then he told me, "You're no different."

"Well, you may be right about that," I replied with a good-natured smile.

I better get on the road. My next town is Del Rio. Route 90 runs right through it and takes me to San Antonio about 150 miles from here.

Sunday, September 21, 2003
Day Twenty-Five: Arrive San Antonio, Texas

But first, I have to gas up. In spite of what the Kawasaki guy said about more rain to the east, I leave without putting on my rain gear. I hate that rain gear, it's hot and uncomfortable. Well, that lasts about twenty miles, so I stop to put on my two-piece rain suit. It's really a piece of shit because the top is now in tethers from flapping in the wind and in hard rain, the bottoms leak and my ass gets wet.

A few miles later, it starts to come down hard. I'm passing through a small town along Route 90 and spot a huge gazebo to my right in the middle of what looks like a public square. So, I stop to get out of the rain and change into my good one-piece rain suit. The problem with the one-piece is that it's tough to get on, especially over a motorcycle jacket with bulky, heavy, armor padding. It's also hot as hell when it's not raining. But I'll tell you one thing, it's good when it's cold, and right now, I'm starting to feel very cold. So, this was a smart decision, I feel warm *and* dry now. It would be even better if I could see clearly, but that's just the nature of riding in the rain. This isn't a big thunderstorm, more like a solid drizzle that gets harder and harder as I increase my speed.

Now I'm riding across the open prairie at 85 mph with a mild crosswind. The rain feels like a minor hurricane. But, I'm warm and dry which feels good, like I'm cheating Mother Nature out of her torment. My hands are wet though, they haven't invented a decent set of waterproof motorcycle gloves yet, at least I've never seen a pair. So, now I'm riding along, trying to see through the rain and spray from the back of trucks and cars, and I'm thinking, 'Wow, no thunder and lighting, that's great.'

But, unlike the Kawasaki guy that high-tailed it north, I have to go this way or I'll never get home. Now, I'm cruising along at 90 and I'm thinking, 'I haven't had a heart palpitation in over a week.' In fact, I'll bet I've had maybe one or two on this whole trip. I usually have them almost every day at home. People like me, with a mitral valve prolapse, get these palpitations in all different degrees. I wonder what's going on with my body while I'm on this motorcycle trip that's different

Sunday, September 21, 2003
Day Twenty-Five: Arrive San Antonio, Texas

than when I'm at home. I don't have a stressful job at home, hell, I don't even have a job, I'm retired.

The thing that's different about traveling by motorcycle is that life is always in the here and now with no past to stew on, no future to worry about. It's all about what's happening right now and staying alive. I think that may be the difference. I make the 150 miles to San Antonio in one piece and find a place to stay within walking distance of Denny's. After throwing my luggage in my room, I walk over for lunch. I'm told, "Sorry, we're closed right now due to a loss of power, try us again in an hour or so." That was my greeting as I entered. I thought it was a little strange that the place looked so dark.

I walk back toward the motel and I see a Mexican restaurant a few blocks down the road. It looks like a shithole from the outside. But, what the hell. I walk down the street and go in. The place is packed with people, Mexican people. I locate a small table in the corner and order a bottle of Tecate, which isn't easy because the waiter doesn't speak English...at all. Next, I try to order some food from the menu, no luck. The waitress is friendly, but I can see in her eyes, she has no idea what I'm talking about. I manage to ask her for someone that speaks English and a few moments later, a nice young fellow comes over to my table. He speaks excellent English. Unfortunately, he has no idea what a burrito is! So, I ask him, "How about something like a burrito, you know, some food wrapped up in a tortilla?" All I get is a blank stare.

Finally, I say "Thank you, I'll just finish my Tecate and go somewhere else." He smiles and leaves. Why do I feel like he was trying to discourage me from eating here? I finish my beer and slowly walk back to my motel, kill some time in my room and walk back to Denny's, hoping that by now, they have their power back on. Great, their computers are up, the lights are on and they're serving food again.

Now, this is weird; I tell the young waiter I want a veggie burger, no cheese. His eyes light up, he smiles real big and says, "That's very good!" Then I ask for a Garden salad, no cheese and again, his eyes light up, he smiles real big and says, "That's very good!" I order dry hash

Sunday, September 21, 2003
Day Twenty-Five: Arrive San Antonio, Texas

browns, the same happy response. I don't say anything though, I just let him take the order. A few minutes later, the young guy comes back with my order. I ask him, "Are you a vegetarian? The reason I ask," I say, "is because you seemed so pleased about every item I ordered."

He smiles again and says, "No, I'm just trying to be happy because I know for a fact that the world is going to end very soon." Then he excuses himself to take care of another customer.

Okay, he's got my interest now. If the world is going to end very soon, I want to know more because this could affect my travel plans. A few minutes later, he comes back to see if I'm doing okay.

"Yes, I'm fine, the food is great," I tell him. "But excuse me please, may I ask you another question?"

"Yes, sure," he answers with a little suspicion in his voice.

Then I ask very politely, "Why do you feel the world is ending very soon?"

"Oh, because of people I've talked to and books I've read," he answers. Now I have to pose the obvious question. So very carefully, I ask, "Is this based on religion or the bible? Because, you know, the bible talks a lot about this subject."

"Yes," he says. "That's one of the books, the other is a book by Jim Marrs."

"Jim Marrs is a prolific writer," I say. "He writes a lot about conspiracies, like the Kennedy assassination. In fact, his book on the Kennedy assassination is one of the books that Oliver Stone based his movie on about President Kennedy's death." The young guy is surprised that I know about Marrs and this gets him even more excited and he starts quoting some writings of Nostradamus. After listening to that for a few moments, I can see where he's coming from and I tell him, "That's fascinating stuff. Keep on reading; the answers are out there." A strange, but charming guy. I enjoy eccentric people.

After I the pay cashier for my lunch and buy gas for my bike, I head back to my room for a rest. An hour later, I'm feeling relaxed and

Sunday, September 21, 2003
Day Twenty-Five: Arrive San Antonio, Texas

ready for new challenges, like doing my laundry; I don't have any more clean clothes. But first, I have to find a motorcycle shop to get some work done on the bike. I can't do it today because it's Sunday, but I want to be there when they open first thing in the morning so I can get in and out as soon as possible. After calling three motorcycle shops in the area, I make a depressing discovery…all the shops are closed on Mondays. Now I recall, this is standard practice all over because these places are open Saturdays, which is a big day, whereas Mondays are usually dead, so they are all closed on Sunday and Monday.

Now what? I call Kathy on my cell phone. I'm surprised she answers. "Hi Kenny, I didn't go to the Dolphins game. I'm so relieved about that! I was busy all day. I washed Eddy, worked on some projects around the house and now I'm just so tired. I'm glad I can just stay home and relax."

"I'm glad things are going your way sweetheart, it's good to hear your voice." Then I tell her, "Guess what? It looks like I'll have to get my bike repairs done on Tuesday because all the bike shops are closed on Mondays, which really sucks. I forgot these places close on Mondays."

She tells me she feels terrible I had to waste a whole day. After my talk with Kathy, I feel better. Maybe I can make the two-hundred miles to Houston in the morning and with a bit of luck, find a bike shop that's open and still get the work done tomorrow. I hate to put it off any longer. Regardless, right now, I have to go over and do my laundry.

One of the things I find really interesting about Texas is that it looks like, well, Texas. With lots of good-old-boys driving pickups. But, unlike the pickups you see in Florida where they're mostly a matter of style, in Texas, the pickups are muddy, dented, scratched up work-trucks hauling horses or machinery. These are real, working pickup trucks. The men driving these pickups either wear baseball caps or cowboy hats, but they always wear a hat. And, the baseball caps have the bill facing the front, I never see them on backwards like in Florida.

Sunday, September 21, 2003
Day Twenty-Five: Arrive San Antonio, Texas

At the little Mexican café in Marfa, where I ate breakfast the other morning, two guys walk in for breakfast. One guy is very tall, about 45, maybe six-feet-four-inches with a bit of a gut on him. He has on worn jeans, muddy boots, a big cowboy hat and he's sporting a walrus mustache. His friend is older, much shorter and rounder with the same outfit and a much bigger gut. They both find a table, sit down and seem to know everyone in the place, except me, of course.

Now, here's the thing, when these two guys talk, they talk with big booming voices. I hear the tall guy bellow at the two guys at the very next table, "Howdy boys, how ya doin' this morning? You boys find any trouble yet today?"
One of the guys at the next table lets out a big hearty laugh and replies in an equally booming voice, "Not yet, but the day is still young. How you boys doin'?" When these two guys get up to leave, the tall
guy hollers out from his table, "You boys take it easy now, see ya later." And so it goes, interesting culture, the South-Texas country life.

Route 90 runs through a lot of tiny towns, well south of I-10, with populations printed on the city limit welcome signs. The populations are usually like 120 and 240. And these little towns never seem to tear anything down, at least not on purpose. That job belongs to mother nature. Hence, all the abandoned stores, houses and barns. They just stand there aging until they fall apart. Marfa is probably an exception because I was told that out-of-staters are buying up property in Marfa in record amounts. Samantha, the barmaid at the El Paisano Hotel, told me, "Some people here think Marfa could become the next Santa Fe."

The Kawasaki guy I talked with this morning confirmed what Samantha said, telling me, "Lots of artsy people are moving there or they're thinking about it. The land values are already zooming up."

But overall, some of the smaller towns in Texas do have a lot of character. And it's real, not Disney-ized for tourism. It's the towns along the secondary roads, off the beaten path that are so fascinating, not the ones along the interstate. These places are a thousand times more

Sunday, September 21, 2003
Day Twenty-Five: Arrive San Antonio, Texas

interesting than the tourist traps like Gatlinburg or even phony-baloney Disney world. You can't duplicate authenticity. This city, San Antonio, where I am right now, is not a small town but it does have all that Texas-Mexico character.

After finishing my laundry, I ride my bike around the area to find a bar. I spot a place called Boozers, A Drinking Establishment. That's close enough for me. I park and walk in. I find a good seat at the corner of the enormous square bar that is the centerpiece of this large country western style saloon. In the rear are several busy pool tables and to my right is a dance floor and a stage for the band. I order a Heineken and tip my bottle as a casual hello to the guy sitting at a right angle to me on the opposite corner of the bar. He seems friendly enough, a young, clean-cut, Mexican looking guy, heavy set, maybe 28 or 30. I ask him if he lives here. He nods yes.

"Do you mind if I ask you a question?" He nods, okay. "I'm just traveling through here from Florida and this afternoon, I stopped into a Mexican restaurant by my motel here in town. I tried to order a burrito and all I got was a blank stare from the waitress. So, my question is, how can they not know what a burrito is?"

"I think that's more an American/Mexican dish, not an authentic Mexican dish," he patiently tells me.

"Well, thanks, I guess that explains it," I tell him. Later, we get to talking a little more and he tells me he's here on a working assignment. He handles the Karaoke entertainment that starts in a few minutes. He says it's his father's business but he likes to do it and it helps his dad. His real job is with Xerox. He's a department manager with them and works with large corporate accounts. A few minutes later, he kicks off the Karaoke by singing a song. The guy is good too.

While I'm enjoying the music, a woman about 40, with a black cowgirl outfit, very wide hips and long blond hair sits down next to me. Her boyfriend sits on the other side of her. The next thing I know, she's up on stage, singing "Crazy," an old Patsy Cline tune. She sounds just like Patsy Cline too. She's good. When she sits down, I tell her, "Wow,

Sunday, September 21, 2003
Day Twenty-Five: Arrive San Antonio, Texas

that was great!" I can tell from her expression she's very pleased. A bit later, she does two more songs and I realize I probably should have kept my opinion to myself because she's really bad. In fact, when she sits down after the two-song bit, she apologizes to me for being so bad. I feel sorry for her after that. It appears she comes here all the time to sing and well, she's just not very good except for the one song, "Crazy." She never did get any better later in the evening. One-song-Sally ran through my mind.

The next thing I realize, the place is packed with people, no more empty bar stools. Now a guy is standing right next to me at the very corner of the bar, drinking a Bud. The guy is just looking around. But there's something different about this guy. He's about six-feet and maybe one-inch tall, he's wearing a black t-shirt and jeans with a huge gold and bronze belt buckle. He has a muscular, wiry build and not an ounce of fat on his body. He's handsome but not pretty-boy handsome like a young Pierce Brosnan, more like the badass Indian brave that leads a charge into the US Calvary and scalps the Colonel. In fact, he looks just like an American Indian.

I notice he stands very straight and proud, his thumbs occasionally resting on his big shiny belt buckle. His eyes are darting around, like a wild animal wary of danger. I'm thinking to myself, this guy is a poster boy for the proud American Indian brave of by-gone times. He knows he's bad and he's just waiting for someone to fuck with him.

But, the guy makes me curious and I've got to see what he's all about, so I tap him lightly on his upper arm to get his attention. Then I ask him, "Hey, how come you don't have a big gut like a normal American, is there something wrong with you?" He turns and stares at me like, who the fuck are you? Then he says, "What do you mean?"

"I mean, how do you stay so fit, do you work out with weights or does it just come naturally?" I reply.

Sunday, September 21, 2003
Day Twenty-Five: Arrive San Antonio, Texas

"I don't lift weights and I don't run. I drink beer all day, starting at about 11AM and every day, I smoke three packs of cigarettes. I guess I'm just lucky."

"Well, whatever you're doing, it's working. Maybe you just have good genes." I say. Then he looks in the other direction to ignore me and I think to myself, 'okay, Ken, so you got lucky and he didn't punch me in the face for asking him a stupid question.' I decide to quit while I'm ahead and keep my mouth shut. Then, a little time passes and he looks over at me and says, "I ride Bulls."

"You mean the phony-baloney bulls in western bars or real bulls?" I ask, putting on a brave front.

"Real Bulls," he says, with a hint of pride. "I've been doing it since I was a kid."

"Shit, that's why you're in such good shape!" I say, showing I'm impressed. Then I add, "That's really hard to do, riding bulls."

"Yeah, I guess it is," he tells me with an expressionless face. "But I like it. It's my hobby, it's what I like to do." Then we shut up again.

A few minutes later, out of the blue, he says to me, "You would not be able to guess what I do for a living." Pausing a moment to ponder his question, I admit I'm stumped, so he tells me, "I run a bodyguard service. I have quite a few tough guys, 250 to 275 pounds, that work for me. They protect important people when they come into town and I get $2,000 to $2,500 per day for the service. Now he's clearly trying to impress me. But, I'm also thinking, no wonder this guy looks like such a badass, that's his job!

There's another long period of silence and he moves to a bar stool that opens about where the Karaoke guy was sitting earlier and next to a tall, thin guy he seems to know pretty well. They make a little small talk. I wait for a pause in their conversation and walk over to my new friend and say to him, "Listen, I need to ask you a question and I'm asking this because I think you're a very intriguing character. Not wanting to make any assumptions about him, I say, "Tell me, what's

Sunday, September 21, 2003
Day Twenty-Five: Arrive San Antonio, Texas

your family heritage, you know, your nationality." Based on his appearance, I knew right after I uttered the words it was not the brightest question I could have asked. He stares at me for a moment, trying to figure me out and finally says "I'm an American Indian, a Comanche from the Blackfoot tribe."

"I was guessing you were an American Indian, but I didn't know what tribe. I just wanted to ask. Then he tells me, "You know, I can be a mean son-of-bitch if anyone pisses me off." Implying, that if you're fucking with me now's a pretty good time to stop. Knowing I better tread carefully, I say, "I believe you. I think you look like one mean motherfucker."

"I am," he quickly confirms.

"But," I tell him, "You're a mean motherfucker with dignity, a sense of pride and a good sense of fair play. I just sense that about you. It shows in the way you carry yourself." Still suspicious, he nods his head to acknowledge what I said was true. Then, looking me in the eye, he tells me he still has a lot of anger for white people and resents that they claim this as white man's country. "The Indians," he says, "my people, got fucked out of our land. Now, we have to live on reservations." I tell him that a lot of us white people have read about the injustices done to the Indians and agree with him.

"My wife and I love the philosophy of the Indians before the white men screwed them," I say sympathetically. "Their respect for Mother Earth, their respect for animals and their way of life, so in harmony with nature, it was beautiful."

"Well, he says, "It's one thing to read and another to live it."

"I believe what you're saying, but reading is all I have to go on at this point. Anyway," I say earnestly, "My wife and I really do love the philosophy of the early Indians. We wish things could have been done differently. There are a lot of us whites that feel this way." I sense he is trying to accept my heartfelt feelings at face value. After a couple more exchanges, his defenses break down and we introduce ourselves. He tells me his name is Johnny and he wants to know

Sunday, September 21, 2003
Day Twenty-Five: Arrive San Antonio, Texas

why I'm so interested in him. He thought maybe I was a writer or reporter

"No, I travel all over the country on my motorcycle," I tell him, "and my hobby is meeting and talking with interesting people...but I gotta say, you're one of the most interesting people I have met." He couldn't resist smiling after my comment. Then he tells me that he earned the big bronze and gold belt buckle for winning a bull riding championship. Later, I buy him a beer "because I love American Indians" I tell him, which I do. Soon, I realize it's almost midnight and I'm starved. So, I say, "Johnny, I better head back to my motel before I'm too drunk to ride my motorcycle."

He gives me a warm handshake, puts his arm around my shoulder and says, "Hey, Ken, if you ever come back, come on a Sunday night. I'll be here. I'd like to see you again." It was nice to hear him say that because he was one of the most challenging and fascinating people I've met on this trip. As soon as I walk out the door, the fresh air wakes up my appetite. Damn, I'm starving. I ride across the street to another Mexican Restaurant. They're getting ready to close. Still, the waiter smiles and allows me in. I'm barely able to communicate in English, but I do get a burrito, no carne, no cheese. They still bring it out with sour cream though. Fuck it, it's too late and I'm too hungry, I scrape off the cream and eat it. In fact, I'm so hungry, I get a second order, this time they leave off the sour cream.

Monday, September 22, 2003
Day Twenty-Six: Arrive Beaumont, Texas

I get a late start this morning because I didn't get to bed until after midnight. I eat breakfast at Denny's. No sign of my eccentric and friendly waiter. Without wasting any time, I'm back on the road. I need to make the two-hundred miles to Houston as fast as possible and look for a motorcycle shop. I make it to Houston in good time, but this is an immense city, overwhelmingly big and the traffic is unbelievable, fuck this. I ride right through Houston. At 3:30, I'm back on I-10 and entering Beaumont, Texas. I get a room at the first motel I see, the Interstate Inn. Then I look through the phone book in my room and call a Honda motorcycle shop. I'm shocked when someone answers the phone. Could I be this lucky to find a shop open on Monday? I ask, "Are you open?"

"Yes, we're open until six o'clock," the woman tells me.

I say, "I'll be right over." I hang up the phone, write down the phone number and address and ask the motel manager how to get there. "It's about 20 miles east on I-10," he says. Well, that's the direction I'm headed in the morning. I've only got two hours until they close, should I just wait 'till morning? Ah fuck it, I'm not doing anything right now, why not take a chance and just go, maybe they'll still have time to slap on a back tire and fix my chain before they close.

With the help of the city map the hotel manager gave me, I arrive at the Honda shop at about five o'clock. They do have a rear tire but no chain that fits my bike. My bike uses an uncommonly heavy-duty chain and they don't stock them. They install the rear tire and adjust and tighten my loose chain. By 6:15, I'm headed back to my motel. That was an excellent decision, I think to myself. Now, I can get right on the road tomorrow morning, no need to stop for repairs. Shit! I forgot to get the oil changed. Oh well, I guess it will just have to wait until I get home, it's not a safety issue. After a couple of beers and a tasty Mexican dinner, I'm in bed by 9:30.

Tuesday, September 23, 2003
Day Twenty-Seven: Arrive Gulfport, Alabama

I get an early start, which is hard for me, but I want to make some miles today. I'm ready to get home now. The weather is beautiful and I surprise myself by getting on the road by 8:30. Ouch! The damned morning sun is shining right in my face. Never-the-less, it's interstate all the way and I'm making good time cruising between 75 and 95mph, depending on conditions. About one hundred miles before hitting Mobile, Alabama, I decide to make it home in a single stretch. I said I wasn't going to do this, but now I'm feeling like a barn horse that wants to go home. I figure I should get in at about 2AM, maybe three at the latest. Hell, I can do that. I stop for gas and a short rest about thirty miles from Pensacola.

I hear some strange noises from the bike, but I can't identify the sound. I checked the chain several times during the four hundred miles I've covered so far today, and it seems okay. But this time when I leave the gas station, I accelerate really hard to merge with traffic and level off at about 95 mph. The bike definitely doesn't feel right, and I slow down to 85 and pay more attention. It feels squirrelly, wandering, like the back tire is following a wavy groove in the road, or it's going flat. I know what a flat feels like. I'm thinking, shit, what now? Maybe my back tire is going flat, I pull over to the side of the interstate and look things over. The tires aren't low on air. I shake the bike with the handlebars as hard as I can and slam my boot into the side of both tires to see if the wheels are loose.

Everything checks out okay. Why the sloppy ride? Then, just for the hell of it, I touch my chain with the toe of my boot. Shit! It's looser than I've ever seen it. That last hard acceleration must have done it in. This bike isn't safe to ride now, I know it. I start the motor and slowly ride it along the shoulder of the Interstate to the next exit. With the help of a gas station attendant, I locate an Alabama Honda dealer, about 26 miles south of where I stopped. Then, I call Triple A and arrange for a tow truck. It's not all that surprising the chain gave out, although that still doesn't explain the wandering I felt in the back end.

Tuesday, September 23, 2003
Day Twenty-Seven: Arrive Gulfport, Alabama

My chain gave out in '97 in Santa Fe, New Mexico, that time the chain gave me plenty of warning, mostly strange noise. This time it's a strange noise, but the squirrelly back wheel is even stranger. I think with mechanical breakdowns you always get some warning first. I haven't heard of anyone dying because their motorcycle spontaneously exploded or a wheel fell off at 100 mph. Motorcycles almost always crash because the rider or a motorist did something stupid. And usually, it's the motorcyclist doing the stupid part. I know, because I've done more than my share of stupid. Anyway, the chain failure could have been dangerous, but I stopped. If I had ignored the signs, I don't know what would have happened. Maybe the back wheel would have locked up. Perhaps the chain would have broken and wrapped around my ankle, ouch! But it gave me lots of clues, so nothing happened.

The tow truck, the kind with a long flatbed for hauling cars, arrives about twenty minutes late, nothing new there. The driver is a young guy with hair down to his shoulders and a thick Alabama accent. Once inside the cab, with the bike secured in back, he tells me he grew up right in this area. He got married fifteen years ago when he was eighteen and he's got two boys. He is a very polite young fellow in the tradition of the old south. He calls me "sir" a lot and says he's not sure if he has a happy marriage.

He says, "I couldn't have a better wife, but we fight and argue a lot." I indicate I'm listening, but keep my mouth shut. It sounds to me he's not happy with his marriage. He probably thinks his wife is a good mother to his kids and maybe something's wrong with him. Just my impression.

Tuesday, September 23, 2003
Day Twenty-Seven: Arrive Gulfport, Alabama

He continues on, telling me "I've never been outside this area except once when I drove to Kentucky to pick up a car and drove it straight back home, didn't really see much."

He wonders what the rest of the world is like and gets bored with the same small town all the time. "I'd like to move around a bit," he tells me. I can understand why, I think to myself, it's the old dilemma of a small-town boy that gets married too young with a nowhere job and kids to support. I don't offer any advice, but continue to listen sympathetically.

While we were loading the bike on the back of his truck, he told me, "I've picked up quite a few sport-bikes like yours, but they were always wrecked, totaled actually, and I never had to worry about how I put them on the back of the tow truck. Yours is the first one that I've had to be careful with." I could sense he wasn't too sure about what he was doing, now I know why.

With my cell phone, I call Kathy from the tow truck and tell her what's going on. She's doing okay and getting ready to fix dinner, then watch a movie she rented for the evening. Next, we drop the bike off at the Honda dealer in Gulfport, Alabama. They're closed so I park the bike under the lights in front of the showroom window, so it would be visible from the street and lock up the front wheel with my brake lock. I figure the lighting will deter theft. The driver drops me off at a motel about a half-mile down the road where I get a great room for $39 a night. I pay him for the tow with a generous tip and wish him well on his marital issues.

From my room, I call the municipal police department and tell them where my bike is parked, why it is there and ask them to keep an eye on it. They probably don't give a shit, but I figure it can't hurt to ask. The only restaurant close by is a steak and ribs place down the street from my motel. Two Heinekens, two baked sweet potatoes, a garden salad, and an order of well-seasoned steamed veggies taste good and fill my belly

Wednesday, September 24, 2003
Day Twenty-Eight: Overnight Gulf Port, Alabama

Nowhere to eat my regular breakfast, so I eat two bowls of the motel's pre-packaged oatmeal, mixed with some hot water along with a couple of bananas topped off with some coffee. At 9AM, I walk the half mile to the Honda shop. I'm thinking to myself that I'm happy I took this trip. It was interesting. I mean the places I saw and the people I met along the way were great. I wonder if I'll ride my motorcycle much when I get home. Chances are I won't. Motorcycling in South Florida isn't that much fun. The idea of taking a long trip with stimulating roads and great conversations over beer and food is my real motivation to ride.

When I get to the Honda shop, my bike is still right where I left it, so I walk it around to the service department. The service manager remembers my phone call from yesterday afternoon. I tell him about the chain and squirrely back wheel. He nods and hands off my trusty Blackbird to Billy, his mechanic for priority service. Billy puts the bike up on the center stand, starts the motor and slowly engages the clutch to get the back wheel turning. Then he says, "Look at this, see the back wheel wobbling?"

"Shit!" I tell him, "That's what I felt when I pulled over on I-10, it felt like a flat tire."

"Yeah," he says, "you need a whole new rear axle, bearings and three or four other related parts. Now, since we're ordering all these axel parts, we may as well order new sprockets too; both front and back look worn

The shop manager enters the scene next and promises to get the parts ordered right now on the computer. "If we can get the parts order in before noon and request overnight delivery, we'll have them by tomorrow morning."

I wander around customer service, while the service manager enters all the parts numbers into the computer, then wait with anticipation while he receives confirmation. He prints out the list and double checks everything just to make sure. He's really trying his best for me. I sure don't feel like spending more than one extra night waiting around for my repairs. "They should be here tomorrow by 9AM," he

Wednesday, September 24, 2003
Day Twenty-Eight: Overnight Gulf Port, Alabama

tells me, and then says, "The cost of the parts is $361. And, of course, the labor is additional." I figure this is going to run about eight hundred and sign the repair authorization. Billy takes me back to my motel and that's it for motorcycling until tomorrow.

When I get back to the motel, I put on my walking shorts for the first time on this trip and begin the three-and-a-half-mile walk to the small, Gulf Port, Alabama resort area on their beach. The walk is pleasant, the sky is clear and the temperature is in the mid-80s. It's a Wednesday, the beach is quiet and pretty with unusually white sand. It's also more expansive and wider than most beaches. The water is placid and the whole scene is quiet and peaceful with plenty of clear blue sky. There are only a few people on the beach. Parked along the beach is a guy asleep behind the wheel of his pickup.

An open-air bar with a big wooden deck is where I stop first for a beer. The place is quiet with one other customer and an aging barmaid who looks like, at one time, she had been quite attractive. I overhear the lone customer ask her, "How can you stand looking at this white sand all day?"

"I've been doing it for eight years," she says without looking up from the sink where she is washing glasses. I wonder to myself, 'where's the problem? This sand is beautiful to look at.' After one beer, I leave and aimlessly walk around to kill time, checking the place out. It's a typical tourist beach, small though, not many establishments. There are a few Jimmy Buffet style drinking places that probably get going pretty good on the weekends. Nothing for me to eat, just burgers, fried fish, clams, shrimp and fries. But then this isn't a vegan resort. I start walking back toward my motel on the main road leading in and out of the beach.

This road is lined with T-shirt shops, palm readers, souvenir shops and more fish restaurants than I care to count. And then, I spot an Internet café. The sign says, Sandwiches. I have a hunch they'll have something I like. Sure enough, two veggie selections on the menu. I order a veggie sandwich with a side of cold pasta with seasoned olive oil. While I'm waiting for my order, I see a big green parrot, not far from where I'm sitting. The parrot is busy jabbering away. The only ones in

Wednesday, September 24, 2003
Day Twenty-Eight: Arrive Gulf Port, Alabama

the shop are the owner/waitress, me and the damn parrot that will not shut up, at least not until the owner yells, "SHUT UP! "

I ask her about her business and how she got started. That was a big mistake; she starts talking…and talking and talking. She was worse than the fucking parrot. Anyway, it turns out she's from Seattle, Washington and came here to be with her mom and dad. Apparently, they moved here from Seattle and then she got lonely. She had heard about the concept of an Internet café and opened one here on the beach. Telling me this tiny bit of information takes her what seems like hours. In between, I manage to order another sandwich and salad and could have eaten another one, but between the talking woman and her squawking parrot, I'd had enough talk for today.

I walk again in the direction of my motel and pass a pizza joint that looks like it has a nice bar. It seems friendly, so I go in and order a Heineken. The husband and wife to my right are talking to the barmaid about TVs, truck tires, and the Lotto. I mostly listen and stare at the TV over the bar. I'm definitely getting bored now. After the husband and wife leave, I swallow the rest of my beer, ask where the men's room is and take a leak in preparation for my three-mile walk back to the motel. The walk back is pleasant and the weather is beautiful.

It's funny how after something happens, all the little clues you got earlier start making sense. The subtle noises and squealing that I couldn't quite put my finger on, the wobbly feel from the rear wheel but no flat tire, the constant chain tightening. One thing was feeding the other. The axle and bearings were destroyed because of all the rain I rode through. Not to mention the fact that the bike has 36,000 miles on it. That's a lot of miles for a motorcycle. Most of them are in the motorcycle graveyard before 36,000 miles.

When I get back to the motel, I order a 14-inch cheese-less veggie pizza and quickly devour the whole damn thing. I could have eaten another one. I think I may have lost a few pounds on this trip because I haven't been snacking and most days, I only eat two meals. I watch the California Governors debate, but after 45-minutes, I give up and channel surf before falling asleep. The debate was more of a

Wednesday, September 24, 2003
Day Twenty-Eight: Arrive Gulf Port, Alabama

shouting match than anything like a real debate. I couldn't take it anymore.

Thursday, September 25, 2003
Day Twenty-Nine: Arrive Tallahassee, Florida

I'm up at 7:45AM and eat the same pre-packaged oatmeal and bananas. I walk to the Honda shop and hope, like a kid waiting for Santa, that my parts arrive on time and I can get out of here early today.

Bingo! At 9AM, Santa arrives in a Fed-X truck with all my parts. The mechanic shows me the old axle bearings and related parts. They look like they had been salvaged from a sunken ship on the bottom of the ocean. The balls had fallen out of the ball bearing retainer ring and all the parts were coated with rust. He says to me, "Man, you must have ridden through one hell of a lot of rain to do this."

"Well," I say, "I thought I did, now I know it wasn't my imagination." At 2:30PM, I leave the Honda shop with my wallet $900 lighter. After filling my belly with a tasty lunch, I load my luggage, pay the motel bill and head back to I-10, about twenty-six miles north of here. It's 3:45PM and the weather is nice. Well, it was nice for a while.

At about 6:30, the whole sky opens up on me. I mean it's coming down in buckets. You know it's raining hard when cars pull over on the shoulder of an interstate highway. Of course, I don't have any rain gear on, so I'm now wet to the bone. To make matters more exciting, this is a lightning storm. I can barely see because both my face shield and eyeglasses are wet and foggy. Quickly, I flip up my face shield, pull my glasses down on my nose to look over them. Now I can at least see well enough to pull over onto the shoulder and stop. Lots of cars are already pulled over and I feel lucky I didn't rear-end one because the visibility was so poor. After resting a minute or so, I get my bearings and spot an overpass about a quarter mile ahead.

I slowly pull out and pass the cars on the shoulder to make my way to the shelter of the overpass. I have visions of being hit by a bolt of lightning at any moment, turning me and my bike into a big fireball. It is a feeling of total vulnerability against the weather gods. As I'm moving to the overpass, 18-wheelers were speeding by on my left, drenching me with spray. Those fuckers don't stop for anything

A late model Buick with two elderly people is already parked under the overpass. As I pull up beside them, the guy opens his window and says something like "Guess it's a bad day for motorcycling, huh?"

Thursday, September 25, 2003
Day Twenty-Nine: Arrive Tallahassee, Florida

I respond, "Well, the water won't kill me, but it sure did ruin my afternoon ride." I'm annoyed. I feel like saying, "FUCK YOU!!" The rain slows a bit and I take off again. I start thinking of that aerospace guy on the Kawasaki and how much he hated to ride in thunderstorms. I'm still concerned about the lightning, but it's incidental to dealing with other more immediate problems, like lack of vision and other vehicles. Plus, I'm soaking wet and getting cold. Stupidly, I refuse to stop and put on my rain suit. I figure I'm already soaked, maybe the air will dry me off if it ever stops raining that is. Well, it does stop, but now I'm cold to the bone and shaking.

I stop and put on my full body, all-weather rain suit. It's a bitch to get on and it's not very comfortable either, but it's dry and warm. That bought me another 105 miles, at which time I hit Tallahassee. It's late in the day and it will soon be dark. I'm getting a motel. I'm uncomfortable, wet and now I'm tired. I take off the one-piece suit as soon as I enter the room. The AC is on full blast and when the cold air hits me, I start shaking again, like I had just crawled out of a frozen lake. So, I quickly turn the heat on full blast and, ah, that feels good.

After a warm shower, I call Kathy to tell her where I am. She and Eddy are fine. I then put on some clean clothes and ride about three miles to a little pizza bar the desk clerk recommended. It's not really in Tallahassee, just in the general area. I'm still very much in the country. It's now turned dark and I'm riding through three miles of North Florida pine forest to find this place. The rain has stopped, but there's a light fog and the humidity is so high, it feels like a light drizzle.

The joint is rustic on the outside. Inside, you couldn't think up a place like this. There is a long bar, three pool tables and a big stage for karaoke. The floor has three different coverings: wood, linoleum and carpet. It's like looking at the evolution of a floor going back a hundred years. There are at least half a dozen kids in the place, including one six-month-old baby. It's the local hang out for sure. The kids just mill around, playing the video games and shooting pool while mom and dad drink and eat. Everyone here has a deep southern accent.

Thursday, September 25, 2003
Day Twenty-Nine: Arrive Tallahassee, Florida

The people are very nice. I get the cook, a friendly, matronly woman to make me a veggie wrap with grilled onions and a bunch of other grilled veggies. It's so tasty, I ordered another one. She tells me since I liked it so much, she's going to add it to the menu. After this, the karaoke starts. The first karaoke singer, a woman, is easy on my ears. I tell her how much I enjoyed her singing and she points out her son to me. "He'll be up soon," she says. "He's really good. He has his own band and they just cut a CD. He's gonna sing a song from his CD and I'll accompany him."

After that conversation, I start talking to the guy sitting next to me at the bar. He tells me the cook that made me the great veggie wrappers is his wife. Then he asks where I'm from and I tell him about the motorcycle trip. He tells me about the 1986 Honda Goldwing he inherited from his brother-in-law. "I loved that bike," he says sadly. "But, an old lady made a left turn in front of me and I crashed it into her car. I cried, I loved that bike so much." I ask him why he never bought another one. "Well," he says, "we recently bought three mobile homes, one for us and one for our kids to get them out of our house. And one for my parents, so I've kind of got myself a little in debt right now."

He's a nice guy. Talking with him makes me realize the difference in the way people live in rural North Florida compared to the suburban Southeast Florida where I live. Money isn't that easy to come by up here. Some things that I take for granted, these people don't have.

Friday, September 26, 2003
Day Thirty: Arrive Home

It's 8:15. I'm up earlier than usual. I'm wondering about what's going on with my left shoulder blade and that area on my back. I've been wearing a small terry cloth towel over that area every day because any wind down my back causes a lot of pain. Mostly though, the pain shows up when I'm tired. It will likely disappear when I get home. After a quick cup of coffee and a bagel with jam, I'm back on the road. I'm hoping like hell I don't get any more rain today. The weather is nice right now, but the road is still wet from rain earlier this morning.

Hurray! I make it to I-75, I thought it would take forever. The sky is now full of threatening clouds. I'm anxious to get home. When I hit the Turnpike in Wildwood, I'll only have another 250 miles to go. Everything is going fine until I reach Fort Pierce. Then all those grey clouds that I watched floating around the sky turn a scary gunmetal grey. A small shower here and there, nothing terrible yet. Maybe my luck will hold out.

Nope, not today. Just north of West Palm Beach, the skies open up big time. I had stopped a few minutes earlier to put on my beaten up old rain jacket. I left off my rain pants, too much hassle, I hate rain gear. But, I'm glad I put on the jacket because when the rain arrives, it arrives as a deluge. The traffic on the turnpike slows down to 35 mph. I'm getting rain inside my helmet and the inside of my face shield is now wet, making it hard to see. I have to look between the raindrops running down the inside of my face shield. The cars slow to a crawl. Fortunately, after about 20 minutes, the rain lifts and believe it or not, the sun comes out. Only in South Florida.

I call Kathy at the West Palm Beach service plaza. She tells me she wants to take Eddy and meet me at the Pompano rest stop. "If I leave right now," she says, "We should both arrive there at the same time." Using my left brain rational mind, I stupidly respond with, "No, honey, what's the point, I'll be home before you know it. Plus, the storm is following me and you may hit it on your way to meet me. Not only that, it's Friday afternoon and the traffic is shitty, are you sure you really want to come?"

Friday, September 26, 2003
Day Thirty: Arrive Home

Kathy sounds wounded. "I thought you might feel that way," she says softly. I could sense the disappointment in her voice and I think, 'Ken, you're acting like an asshole. Why try to poke a hole in Kathy's balloon?' This is loving emotion, not an exercise in practical decision making. It's Kathy's effort to make my return home a fun thing? So, I say, "I'm sorry, Kath, I'm being an asshole. Of course, that's a great idea. I can't wait to see you and Eddy. We can follow each other home."

The whole thing works out fine. Kathy is waiting for me at the Pompano rest stop when I show up. It feels great to see her pretty face and hug her slender body again. Excitedly, she gives me a big kiss on the cheek. I say, "What's that, no kiss on the lips?"

"I just now put on fresh lipstick, so I'd look nice for you," she tells me.

"Fuck the lipstick!" We both smile and her sweet lips touch mine while we embrace again. After 30 days it feels so good to be home and back with my baby.

After we disengage from our embrace, I look for Eddy. He's standing behind Kathy and not sure what to do. "Eddy! Hi, how's my main man?" I give him a big smile and he gets excited, prancing around in small circles. Then, he nuzzles his long snout deep into my crotch as only greyhounds do. I kneel down and give him a big hug, thinking to myself, one small, happy family together again. It's good to be away from our loved ones sometimes because it makes you appreciate them so much more when you return…End

Made in the USA
Columbia, SC
19 March 2019